Acing

Tort Law

Second Edition

A Checklist Approach to Tort Law

Shubha Ghosh

*Vilas Research Fellow and
Professor of Law*

*University of Wisconsin
Law School*

Series Editor
A. Benjamin Spencer

A Thomson Reuters business

Mat #41240240

© 2009 Thomson Reuters
© 2012 Thomson Reuters
610 Opperman Drive
St. Paul, MN 55123
1–800–313–9378

Printed in the United States of America

ISBN: 978–0–314–27997–2

Acknowledgements

This project benefited from the support of former students and colleagues. Thanks first to Ayse Guner, SMU Dedman School of Law Class of 2008, and Timothy Martin, SMU Dedman School of Law Class of 2011, for excellent editing and proofreading skills. Former students from my Torts class, they showed their knowledge of the field as well as their expertise in close reading and editing. The materials presented here went through classroom testing through several iterations of the Torts class first at Georgia State College of Law and then at SMU Dedman School of Law. Thanks to the students in these classes for their questions and patience. Finally, thanks to Louis Higgins and the colleagues from Thomson-West for letting me go forth with this project and for providing a home for my classroom materials that have been developed over the years.

Table of Contents

Introduction

Torts is the subject first year students either hate or love. Baffling cases involving, among other things, meat hooks, falling planks, burning hayricks, flying barrels, childish kicks to the shins, and, as one of my former students described "railroads gone wild"—all lead to frustration for law students, especially those seeking a sense of what one needs to know to master the subject of Torts. Despite all appearances, there is something to Torts and appreciating the challenge the subject provides to legal reasoning, policy analysis, and understanding legal process is the first step in mastering the field. This book is designed to make you understand the structure of Torts and help you see that Torts law is about more than railroads, falling scales, or other sources of personal injury. Studying Torts is about understanding the common law process and the litigation system, with all its frustrations and successes.

My goal is to provide you a set of guidelines by which to identify and analyze Torts problems. The guidelines, which often can be reduced to checklists, will help you not only succeed in Torts exams and in most classroom discussions but will also sharpen your legal reasoning skills and identify Torts-related issues in more advanced courses and in actual legal practice. This book is not a treatise on Torts doctrine or on the history of the field. Several excellent books approach Tort law from those angles. Instead, you should think of this study aid as a "how to" book. Specifically, its aim is to show you "how to" approach Torts issues as they come up in the various legal problems you will encounter in a first-year Torts class and beyond.

How should you use this book? Many of you may have bought this book upon realizing that there is a final exam in the course and that exam is tomorrow. Others may have been more diligent, but remain baffled by what you are expected to get out of the course. Others, still, may feel supremely confident that Torts really is a piece of cake and picked up this book as a test of what they know. Whatever scenario describes your situation, this book is designed to provide some clarity to your understanding of the subject. This book is not a substitute for your class, for reading cases, or attending your professor's lecture. It is a supplement to all of these activities and more. Think of this book as a road map or a travel guide, neither of which substitutes for actually going out and experiencing the real sights of the road or wherever your travel destination might be.

One thing this book does not substitute for is what your professor says in class and might tell you will be on the exam. Your professor's instruction is still the best and should be the primary guidepost for how to prepare for the exam. But this book can help you navigate through some of the roadblocks that you come across in your study of Torts. Not all professors will cover all the materials presented in this book. Some professors will skip intentional torts. Almost all will skip business torts or defamation. It is certain, however, that all professors will cover negligence, the backbone of the U.S. Torts system. Nonetheless this book covers a wide range of Torts, just in case your class covers those materials. Very likely, more advanced courses in Torts or upper level courses will cover a lot of the materials presented in these pages, but not discussed in your first year Torts class. You have bought a book that has value beyond the first year of law school. But to get the best value out of the first year class, however, check to see what subjects your first year class covers and then turn to the corresponding chapters in this book to provide some guidance.

This book is structured as follows. Chapter One provides an overview of Torts, presenting the main ideas and policies that percolate throughout the field. The goal of Chapter One is to provide a big picture outline of how to approach a Torts problem, a discussion of the principle policies that underlie Tort law, and a discussion of how Tort law relates to other areas you will encounter in your first year courses: contracts, property, criminal law, and civil procedure. The goal is to help you see how Torts fits into your study of law broadly and also to highlight the major issues that come up in the field. As you will find, Torts cases often present fact situations in which both sides can provide arguments for their position under the law. One of your jobs as a burgeoning attorney is to identify and discuss these positions in terms of the black letter law that a case or a statute tries to provide. However, the resolution of a Torts dispute, especially when both sides may have plausible doctrinal arguments, requires you to go to the next level of policy to argue who has the better case. Chapter One presents the broad policy arguments that arise in Torts and provides a checklist approach to recognizing these policy arguments and articulating them.

The rest of the book provides a "how to" guide for different doctrinal areas of Tort law. Chapter Two presents intentional torts (and defenses to intentional torts). Chapters Three through Six present the law of negligence. Chapter Seven presents the law of strict liability. Intentional torts, negligence, and strict liability are the three categories of tort claims that a plaintiff can rely on to obtain recovery for injury. One of the skills you will learn is how to make arguments for treating a tort claim as an intentional tort claim, a negligence claim, or a strict liability claim. Chapter Eight turns to the subject of remedies. Once a plaintiff establishes a legal entitlement to recover for an injury because the defendant has committed an intentional tort, negligent tort, or a strict liability tort (or some combination of these three), then the plaintiff can obtain a remedy for the conduct of the defendant. Chapter Eight explains what these remedies are. Chapter Nine moves to more specialized topics in negligence and strict liability, specifically the question of defenses that a defendant has to the tort claims raised by the plaintiff. Chapter Ten presents the subject of vicarious liability, which deals with questions of when an employer is liable for the torts committed by an employer or a parent for the torts committed by a child. Finally, Chapters Eleven, Twelve, and Thirteen present three areas of advanced torts: Products Liability, Reputation Based Torts (such as defamation), and Business Torts. These three areas bring together many of the issues discussed throughout the book and show how the Torts building blocks work together in some more advanced and practical areas.

That is how this road map is put together. Now let us unfold it and get a sense of how the world of Torts is laid out.

CHAPTER 1

Overview

HOW TO APPROACH A TORTS PROBLEM

Identifying a Torts problem is relatively simple. The fact pattern you are given indicates that some injury has occurred to a person or to property owned by a person. The person injured seeks to obtain monetary recovery from the person or persons who allegedly caused the injury In order to make a successful recovery, the injured party needs to show why the person or persons who allegedly caused the injury are legally responsible and the amount of the damages. Once you recognize this fact pattern, you know that you will analyze the legal issues as a matter of Tort law.

There are three broad issues you need to address in order to analyze this problem more deeply: the standard of care for liability, the cause of action, and potential remedies.

(1) Standard of care for imposing liability on the defendant: There are three under Tort law. A personal is liable because they (a) intended to harm the party injured, (b) acted in a negligent manner that caused harm to the plaintiff, or (c) caused the injury. These three standards of care correspond to the three types of Torts: intentional torts, negligence, and strict liability. The plaintiff has to show one of these three types of torts has been committed in order to be successful, but a good analysis of a Torts problem will try to find arguments under all three standards of care, in order to cover one's bases and be complete.

(2) Cause of action under each standard of care: Each standard of care provides a basis for causes of action under Tort law. Intentional torts include seven separate causes of action (battery, assault, false imprisonment, trespass to land, trespass to chattel, conversion, and intentional infliction of emotional distress). These causes of action share the requirement that the defendant must have had intent in order to be found liable. The standard of care of reasonableness provides the basis for the cause of action of negligence, which requires the plaintiff to show that defendant owed the plaintiff a duty, that the defendant breached that duty through unreasonable conduct, and that the breach caused the plaintiff to suffer compensable damages. Finally, strict liability imposes liability on the defendant even if he did not have the intent to cause harm or did not act unreasonably. Strict liability provides a cause of action in three instances: injuries from dangerous animals, injuries from ultra-hazardous activities, and injuries from defective products.

(3) Remedies: Once the injured party shows that the defendant is liable under one of the causes of action under Tort law, the plaintiff establishes how the defendant can remedy the violation of the law through payment of monetary damages. Under Tort law, monetary damages have two components: compensatory and punitive. In addition, there are rules for allocating compensatory damages among multiple defendants in situations where more than one party may be liable to the plaintiff.

Whenever you answer a Torts question, make sure you address each of these three major issues. As you progress through the readings in the rest of this book, you will see how the various materials fit in as sub-issues under each of these major issues.

POLICIES UNDERLYING TORT LAW

Two policies underlie tort law: compensation of injured parties and deterrence of harmful conduct. Each of the three major issues can be understood in terms of these two policies.

First, the standard of care recognizes that an injured party should be compensated when someone intentionally harmed him, negligently harmed him, or caused him harm regardless of intent or negligence. One question you may have is why there are three standards of liability of Tort law to compensate injured parties. Why not just simply compensate anyone who is injured? The answer is that Tort law requires compensation from another private party by imposing a legal obligation on that party to compensate the victim. But a party who is required to pay may wonder what they, in fact, did wrong and why they are being forced by the law to compensate the victim. On this point, the deterrence goal of Tort law comes into play. Tort law forces a defendant to compensate an injured party if the defendant intended to harm the the party or the party's property or acted negligently and as a result harmed the the party. Tort law seeks to deter intentional or negligent behavior by individuals and therefore requires compensation as a means of deterring such undesirable conduct.

The deterrence goal also explains why strict liability is a standard of care used to impose liability. First, U.S. tort law has been careful in not imposing liability simply because someone caused harm to someone else unless there has been intentional or negligent conduct. Strict liability has generally been viewed as unfair as a basis for imposing liability on a person, requiring him to compensate an injured party. Second, U.S. Tort law recognizes that there are times when imposing strict liability on a person may be fair and also necessary to deter certain conduct. Therefore, U.S. law has limited the imposition of strict liability to three situations: the maintenance of dangerous animals, ultra-hazardous activities, and products liability. In each instance, the law seeks to deter undesirable conduct even if the defendant has not acted with intent or negligence. We will explain each of these three exceptions to the general rule against strict liability in Chapters Seven and Eleven.

Furthermore, each of the causes of action under Tort law can be understood in terms of the policy goals of compensation and deterrence. Intentional torts include seven causes of action. Each is designed to compensate a person for intentional harm to the body, emotions, and property, both real and personal. Each cause of action is also designed to deter intentional conduct that results in such harm. Similarly, the negligence cause of action compensates for harm resulting from unreasonable conduct and deters such conduct. Finally, as discussed in the previous paragraph, strict liability compensates for and deters conduct in specific areas where we are particularly concerned about harm to the plaintiff: dangerous animals, abnormally dangerous activities, and products liability.

Finally, the structure of remedies also is designed around the policies of compensation and deterrence. A plaintiff can recover only certain types and amounts of damages as compensation. Furthermore, punitive damages are recoverable only in certain situations and under certain guidelines. The rules governing compensatory and punitive damages are designed to compensate for certain types of injuries and to deter certain undesirable conduct under Tort law.

A FEW WORDS ABOUT LAW AND ECONOMICS

It is likely that your Torts class might emphasize or at least mention law and economics analysis as applied to the issues of compensation and deterrence. At a very broad level, there are two parts to the law and economics analysis of Tort law. The first is in support of Tort liability and states that if one person causes harm to another, then the person causing harm should compensate the injured party. This argument is often referred to as "cost internalization." The second part of the analysis is in opposition to Tort liability and states that if the law incorrectly imposes liability on a person then beneficial conduct may be deterred. Here is a simple example of each. If a company puts a harmful product on the market that injures people, then the company should compensate the injured parties in order to internalize the cost of the harmful actions. By internalizing costs, victims will be compensated and the company will be deterred from putting harmful products in the marketplace. However, if the law incorrectly imposes liability on the company, then tort liability has deterred beneficial conduct. Therefore, the rules of tort law need to be carefully balanced, according to law and economics, in order not to discourage beneficial conduct. How this balance is to be struck is a difficult question and often will depend on the context. For your purposes, in analyzing Torts problems, you should be aware of these standard arguments in analyzing the policy issues that arise in Tort law.

You may also encounter the Coase Theorem in the context of law and economics analyses of Tort law. According to the Coase Theorem, the injured party and the person causing the injury may get together to negotiate on how to compensate for the injury. Therefore, tort law should be designed with these negotiations in mind. Suppose that the parties could negotiate without any cost. Then, according to the Coase Theorem, the parties will negotiate to the most efficient solution for compensating the victim. The actual Tort rule does not matter if the parties can negotiate without cost because they can always negotiate around the rule. According to the Coase Theorem, Tort law matters only when the parties cannot negotiate because the law permits the victim to obtain compensation that he could not otherwise obtain by negotiating with the person who caused the harm. In situations where negotiation is costly (that is, transaction costs are high), Tort law should be designed to give the plaintiff what he would have obtained through negotiations with the defendant in a hypothetical world where transaction costs are zero and negotiation can occur without cost. Anything less or more than that amount would lead to either underdeterrence or overdeterrence of the defendant's conduct.

You should be aware of the Coase Theorem and what it says generally. You should see how it relates to law and economic policy analysis more broadly. But you should also be aware that the law and economics analysis focuses largely on the efficiency of Tort law, that is, on the effects of Tort law on making society as wealthy as possible. There is no consideration of fairness. As a result, many policy analyses have emerged as a criticism of law and economics that points to the role of Tort law in promoting fairness and social justice. For example, some argue that victims of accidents tend to be poor, members of underrepresented minorities, or women and therefore Tort liability should be responsive to the concerns of these groups. Some law and economics thinkers have responded to these arguments by saying that it is better to resolve issues of fairness and justice through policies other than Tort law, such as civil rights legislation or welfare policies. Again, you should be aware of these arguments. And although there is no clear right or wrong answer to these policy concerns, they inform the debate over Tort law and should inform any policy analysis that you are asked to provide on an exam or in class.

RELATIONSHIP BETWEEN TORTS AND OTHER AREAS OF THE LAW

It is a smart idea to understand how Tort law relates to other areas of the law you are studying. This question is important because the various areas of law do overlap, as you will see in your studies. This section provides some brief comments on this overlap.

Tort law and Contracts: Contract law, like Tort law, is about remedying injury. The difference is that Contract law remedies a very specific type of injury—that arising from the breach of a promise. Tort law is sometime described as recovery for non-contractual-based harm. That is not a bad description (although as we will see in Chapter Thirteen, Business Torts may be the exception to this rule). While all injuries can be divided into those remedied by Tort and those remedied by Contract, it is often the case that Tort law and Contract law can overlap, specifically in the area of Products Liability—the area of law dealing with harm from a defective product. If John buys a toaster from Company A, and the toaster fails to function properly and injures John, then John has a claim for breach of contract against Company A as well as claims for negligence and strict products liability. The remedies for the Contract claims and Tort claims differ, but as we will see, strict products liability in Tort law had its roots in beach of warranty in Contract. In the case of products liability, Contract law and Tort law are not separate, but work together to provide recovery for injured customers of defective products.

Tort law and Criminal law: Criminal law deals with punishment by the state for socially harmful conduct. There are two ways that Criminal law differs from Tort law. First, Criminal law is not concerned with the monetary compensation of victims. Second, Criminal law involves suits brought by the state rather than a suit brought by one private citizen against another. In practice, however, Criminal law and Tort law do overlap. In the area of negligence per se, a way of showing breach of duty in a negligence action, violation of a criminal (or regulatory) statute can be evidence of unreasonable conduct by the defendant. In most states, violation of the criminal statute creates a presumption of unreasonable behavior, or negligence per se. In this way, Criminal law and Tort law can be closely related with a criminal statute setting the standard for unreasonableness under the doctrine of negligence per se.

Tort law and Property law: Some of the rules you will discuss in Tort law may also appear in Property law, particularly trespass and nuisance. Both trespass and nuisance are discussed in this book although the discussion of nuisance is presented as a comparison with trespass. It is not surprising that these doctrines are studied both in Torts and Property since they deal with injury to property. Tort law and Property law are related not only because they both deal with property issues, but also because both are about individual rights—particularly the right to be free from intrusive actions by third parties, or in more familiar terms, the right to exclude. A difference between the two, however, is that Tort law deals with injuries that can be compensated with money damages while Property law focuses on injunctive remedies as well as money damage remedies. This reflects an important difference between the two areas of law. Tort is concerned with the compensation for and deterrence of injuries to rights. Property, on the other hand, focuses on rights of ownership and the transfer of rights through sales, gifts or other forms of distribution.

Tort law and Civil Procedure: Next to Torts, Civil Procedure tends to be the most frustrating course for the first year student. So it should not be surprising that there is a relationship between the two. Both courses provide an introduction to civil litigation. Torts provides a snapshot of how rules develop through common law process and trials. Civil Procedure teaches the rules by which courts to operate, manage, and decide legal claims. More subtly, many Tort rules can be understood with appreciation of the background Civil Procedure rule. For example, the negligence doctrine of res ipsa loquitur allows the plaintiff to claim that the defendant acted unreasonably simply by pointing to the circumstances of the accident. Res ipsa loquitur is an old doctrine going back to the Nineteenth Century when Civil Procedure rules were very different from what they are now. As the rules of Civil Procedure have become more liberal and discovery has become more prevalent, the doctrine of res ipsa loquitur has gone out of favor, requiring the plaintiff to bring in some evidence of unreasonable conduct on the part of the defendant other than the accident itself.

 CHECKLIST FOR OVERVIEW

In addressing Tort questions make sure you consider the big picture in analyzing a fact pattern and writing your answer.

A. Keep in mind the three big questions:

    1. Standard of Care: intent, negligence, or strict liability.

        a. These three are not mutually exclusive. You should consider how each apply to the same fact pattern.

    2. Cause of action: what is the tort cause of action that the plaintiff must prove in order to obtain a remedy from the defendant.

        a. Intentional tort: seven distinct causes of action might apply—battery, assault, false imprisonment, trespass to land, trespass to chattel, conversion, and intentional infliction of emotional distress.

        b. Negligence: plaintiff must show duty, breach, causation, and compensable damages.

        c. Strict liability: arises in three distinct situations:

            (i) Dangerous animals.

            (ii) Ultra-hazardous activities.

            (iii) Strict products liability.

B. Tort Policy

    1. Compensation of injured party.

    2. Deterrence of party from conduct that causes injury.

    3. Law and economics:

        a. Internalization of costs.

        b. Avoid deterrence of beneficial conduct.

        c. Coase Theorem: parties will negotiate to recover harm and therefore if transaction costs are low, tort law is irrelevant. However, if transaction costs are high, then tort law should try to impose liability and damages the way the parties would if they could negotiate.

    4. Criticism of Law and Economics:

        a. Fairness, not efficiency, is goal of Tort law.

        b. Tort law should try to pursue justice by compensating victims who are underprivileged or otherwise underrepresented because of race or gender.

CHAPTER 2

Intentional Torts: Prima Facie Case and Defenses

GENERAL APPROACH

In addressing an intentional tort problem, you need to focus on three major issues. The first is showing that the defendant's conduct meets the legal standard for intent. The second is showing that the defendant's conduct would constitute one or more of the seven causes of action that make up the intentional torts. Keep in mind that the standard for intent is the same for all seven intentional torts, but that the intentional torts differ in terms of the elements and the type of injury each remedies. In general, the seven intentional torts can be divided into personal injury torts and property torts. The personal injury torts are battery, assault, false imprisonment, and intentional infliction of emotional distress. The property torts are trespass to land, trespass to chattels, and conversion. The third issue is that of defenses a defendant can raise to avoid liability for an intentional tort. Remember the three major issues for intentional torts in this way:

(1) Does the defendant meet the standard for intent?

(2) Which of the intentional torts apply to the defendant's conduct?

(3) Does the defendant have any defenses to the intentional tort claim?

ANALYZING INTENT

In all seven intentional tort claims, the plaintiff must show that the defendant had intent. It is important to remember that intent under tort law is very different from intent in criminal law. Under the criminal law, the defendant must have had a guilty mind. In tort law, we are not concerned with moral guilt or culpability. Instead, tort law is concerned with a much narrower and concrete problem: did the defendant act in a way that shows a purpose to cause a consequence or knowledge that a consequence will very likely occur? This approach is consistent with both the compensation and deterrence goals of tort law. The plaintiff can legally force compensation for injury from a defendant who had purpose or knowledge about a bad consequence that is legally sanctioned. It is fair and efficient for tort law to require such compensation because the injury resulted from no fault of the plaintiff, but from the defendant's purposeful or knowledgeable conduct. Furthermore, by making the defendant compensate the plaintiff for purposeful or knowledge-based conduct, tort law deters the defendant from undertaking such conduct in the first place.

The first thing to get straight is that the purpose or knowledge is closely connected to the consequences of each of the intentional torts. Tort law does not make a defendant liable simply for having a bad purpose. Liability is based on the purpose (or knowledge) of a consequence that is covered by one of the seven intentional torts. To illustrate, consider the tort of false imprisonment. It requires intentional confinement of a person against the person's will and with the person's awareness of the confinement. What does it mean for the defendant to intend the confinement? A plaintiff can show intent under tort law in one of two ways.

First, a plaintiff may show conduct by the defendant that indicates a purpose on the part of the defendant to confine the plaintiff. Extreme examples would be tying the plaintiff with rope or locking the plaintiff in a room. More subtle examples might be locking the doors of a car that the defendant and plaintiff are in so that the plaintiff cannot escape. Another example would be driving the car quickly so that the plaintiff cannot get out of the moving car without possibly incurring great injury. Notice that what all of these examples have in common is that the defendant acted in a deliberate way and that deliberate conduct had the consequence of confining the plaintiff.

Second, the plaintiff can establish intent in cases when the defendant had knowledge that confinement could occur with substantial certainty, which you can understand as the legal language for extremely likely. Suppose the defendant asked the plaintiff to step into a room whose door lock was broken so that when the door closed, the room was locked tight. The defendant knew this information about the door and then swung the door closed quickly, locking the plaintiff in. The defendant may argue that his purpose was simply to close the door and not to confine the plaintiff. But if the plaintiff can show that the defendant had the knowledge of the circumstances of the door lock, then there is a strong case for intent under these facts.

Intent in tort law can be shown in one of two ways, either through deliberate conduct, causing certain consequences, or through knowledge that certain consequences would occur with substantial certainty. One case you might read that illustrates the difference between these two ways of showing intent is *Garratt v. Dailey*, 279 P.2d 1091 (Wash. 1955), in which a young boy pulled a chair out from under a grown woman. It was not clear from the facts whether the young boy's purpose was to pull the chair out or to pull the chair in and help the grown woman. But the woman was able to show that the boy's conduct showed knowledge with substantial certainty that the woman would miss the chair and fall to the ground. Therefore, the court found that the boy had acted with intent under tort law.

One issue that arises is whether a court requires that a defendant intended the conduct or intended the injury. Most jurisdictions require that the defendant intended the conduct, but not the injury. So if a plaintiff suffers an unpredictable injury as a result of the conduct then the defendant is liable for the intentional tort. For example, in *Vosburg v. Putney*, 50 N.W. 403 (Wisc. 1891), a school boy kicked the shin of a classmate which resulted in the classmate suffering aggravated injuries because of a pre-existing condition. The kicker was found liable for an intentional tort. A few jurisdictions require dual intent, that is, intent for both the conduct and the injury. But dual intent jurisdictions are rare, and as a result, intentional torts can result in substantial liability for defendants in some situations.

As a further illustration of how intent works in tort law, consider the defense of insanity. From newspapers, you may be familiar with the defense of insanity in criminal cases. In your criminal law class, you will discuss the insanity defense in greater detail. Insanity, however, is not, in general, a defense in tort law. As long as the plaintiff can show that the defendant acted either deliberately or with knowledge that the consequences would occur with substantial certainty, then the defendant's mental state is irrelevant. Suppose a defendant is delusional and thinks the plaintiff is trying to kill him. If the defendant confines the plaintiff in a room, then the defendant is liable for false imprisonment. His delusional state is irrelevant to the fact that he intentionally confined the plaintiff against his will and with his awareness. The defendant has committed the intentional tort of false imprisonment.

ELEMENTS OF INDIVIDUAL INTENTIONAL TORTS

There are seven intentional torts. Each intentional tort covers a different type of injury. When you are analyzing a fact pattern on an exam or in class, try to think of which specific intentional tort is relevant, keeping in mind that more than one may be implicated by the facts. The seven intentional torts break down into two categories: torts involving injury to the person and those involving injury to property.

There are four torts involving injury to the person: battery, assault, false imprisonment, and intentional infliction of emotional distress. Of these four, battery involves injury to the body and the remaining four involve injury to emotions and one's sense of personal dignity.

A battery occurs when a person intends to cause a harmful or offensive touching to the person of another and such harmful or offensive touching occurs. The defendant needs to intend the touching, but not intend harm or offense. A few jurisdictions adopt a dual intent approach and require intent both as to touching and to the harm or offense. Harm can be any physical injury, even a very minimal one. A touching is offensive if it would be deemed offensive by a reasonable person under the circumstances. The reasonableness standard means that offensiveness is based on the circumstances and the customs and norms of the community where the touching occurred. As we will see when we talk about reasonableness in the context of negligence, there is debate about whether reasonableness depends on the gender or other personal traits of the plaintiff. In most jurisdictions, reasonableness is based on a purely objective standard that is often not individualized to the characteristics of the plaintiff, although gender may be relevant in some situations. But if a person is easily offended by being touched, that subjective feeling will be largely irrelevant to the reasonableness analysis.

Assault requires intent as to either causing a harmful or offensive touching or causing immediate apprehension of a harmful or offensive touching. In addition, the plaintiff must have an immediate apprehension of a harmful or offensive touching. Notice that an assault can occur in one of two ways. First, a defendant intended to touch a plaintiff, but missed, causing the plaintiff to feel an immediate apprehension of being touched. Second, the defendant intended to cause immediate apprehension of being touched and the plaintiff felt that immediate apprehension. In the first instance, the defendant intended to commit a battery but missed. If the defendant had actually succeeded in touching the plaintiff, then the defendant would be liable for a battery, but not an assault. The assault merges into a battery if the battery is successful. So be careful of breaking the facts down too finely and concluding that the defendant committed both an assault and a battery when a defendant hits a plaintiff. It is really liability for an assault or a battery in tort law.

Assault poses several interesting challenges because of the requirement of immediate apprehension by the plaintiff. Suppose the defendant sneaks up behind the plaintiff, intending to touch him, but the plaintiff does not notice and the defendant does not touch. Then there is no liability for assault because the plaintiff did not have any immediate apprehension. Even if the defendant comes up to the plaintiff later and says, "I snuck up behind you today and almost touched you," there is no liability for assault unless there is the immediate apprehension by the plaintiff. The same applies if the defendant comes up to the plaintiff and says: "Sometime in the future I am going to touch you harmfully or offensively." Such talk of future touching does not give rise to immediate apprehension. Threats, for similar reasons, do not lead to assault liability unless the threat is of an immediate nature, such as "Your money or your life." In this last case, the immediacy of the threat is held to lead to immediate apprehension and therefore assault liability. Notice that if after the threat the defendant also hits the plaintiff, the defendant would be liable for the assault, based on the threat, and for the battery, based on the hitting. The assault and battery claims would be based on two separate acts by the defendant: the verbal threat and the hitting.

False imprisonment, mentioned briefly above in our discussion of intent, is a tort against one's sense of personal dignity and autonomy. To be liable for false imprisonment, the defendant must intend to confine a person against that person's will and with that person's awareness of the confinement. The confinement must be complete with no reasonable possibility of escape by the plaintiff. If escape is possible only with harm to the plaintiff, to property, or to third parties, then the confinement is complete. Notice that if the plaintiff is not aware of the confinement, then there is no liability. If the defendant knocks the plaintiff unconscious, transports the plaintiff in the trunk of a car back to the plaintiff's home where he is tucked safely in bed to wake up later, there is no liability for false imprisonment (because of lack of awareness of the confinement), but there is liability for battery. A difficult case is presented by a situation in which the plaintiff could have escaped (because the defendant left the plaintiff alone), but felt psychologically confined and unable to leave. Most jurisdictions would very likely find false imprisonment under these circumstances.

Intentional infliction of emotional distress is a relatively recent tort that covers emotional injury suffered by the plaintiff. Courts crafted this tort to deal with situations that would not otherwise be covered by tort law. This tort applies when a defendant intentionally caused severe emotional distress in a plaintiff through extreme and outrageous conduct. The emotional distress must be established through medical or psychological testimony. Extreme and outrageous conduct is determined with respect to community standards and norms of conduct. As an example, consider the case of the defendant who continually threatens plaintiff with harmful physical conduct in the future. Since there is no immediate apprehension, the defendant would not be liable for an assault. But if these continuous threats caused severe emotional distress, then intentional infliction of emotional distress would be an appropriate tort to pursue. In the example above of the unconscious plaintiff locked in the trunk, if the trauma of the attack and the confinement caused severe emotional distress, then intentional infliction of emotional distress may be appropriate.

The remaining three torts cover injury to property. Trespass to land deals with real property; trespass to chattels and conversion, with personal property. Each of these torts reflect the right of a property owner to exclude others from possessing or using her property. Trespass to land occurs when a defendant (a) intentionally enters, or causes a thing or a third party to enter, the land in possession of another, (b) intentionally remains on the land after permission to be on the land is removed, or (c) intentionally fails to remove from the land an item that the defendant is obligated to remove. Trespass to chattel occurs when a defendant (a) intentionally dispossessed another person of personal property or (b) intentionally used or intermeddled through physical contact with the personal property in possession of another. Finally, conversion occurs when a defendant intentionally exercises dominion or control over the personal property of plaintiff so as to seriously interfere with the right of the plaintiff to control the personal property. One key distinction among these three to remember is that trespass to land does not require any harm to the real property to occur for liability to arise. Both trespass to chattels and conversion do require the plaintiff to show harm to the personal property.

The distinction between trespass to chattels and conversion is often a difficult one to understand. In the abstract, trespass to chattels is a tort against rights of possession while conversion is a tort against rights of ownership. Concrete examples may clarify the distinction. Suppose I take someone's suitcase at the airport thinking it looks like mine. I return it after discovering the mistake. I have committed a tort, and it is the tort of trespass to chattels because my intentional act of taking the suitcase deprived the true owner of possession. However, if I realize the mistake and keep the suitcase as if I owned it, then I have committed the tort of conversion. To take another example, suppose I key someone's car, ruining the paint job. Then I have committed the tort of conversion, but not trespass to chattels since the owner of the car still has possession. My act of keying, however, exercised dominion and control over the car in violation of the true car owner's ownership rights.

These are the seven intentional torts. Whenever you encounter an intentional tort problem, make sure to run through all seven of them to make sure you recognize all that apply. To keep them straight, break them down as they are presented here and sort through first torts against the person and second torts against property.

DEFENSES TO INTENTIONAL TORTS

The defendant can raise several defenses against a plaintiff's claim of an intentional tort. These defenses apply to all the intentional torts. Remember that the defendant has the burden to raise and prove these defenses. The five defenses to remember are (1) consent, (2) defense of self, (3) defense of others, (4) defense of property, and (5) necessity.

Consent applies when the plaintiff agreed to defendant's conduct that resulted in the intentional tort. The agreement can be express (such as through a contract) or implied through the conduct of the plaintiff. Consent has boundaries, and if the defendant's conduct goes beyond these boundaries, then consent does not apply. The scope of consent depends on the facts and circumstances of the case and the standards of society for the behavior at issue. In addition, a plaintiff's consent must be informed. If consent is obtained by trickery or force, then the defense does not apply. The amount of information necessary is based on what a reasonable person would need to know in order to agree to defendant's conduct. A defendant can raise the defense of consent if a reasonable person would have believed that the plaintiff had consented and the defendant in fact did believe that plaintiff had consented.

Defense of self allows a defendant to use reasonable force if the defendant reasonably believes that the plaintiff is about to commit harmful conduct on the defendant. The threatened conduct can be any type of tort: intentional, negligent, or strict liability. For force to be reasonable, it must not be disproportionate to the threatened harm. Deadly force is reasonable only if the threat reasonably appears to be deadly or of serious bodily harm. Courts are split on whether the defendant is required to retreat. Some jurisdictions hold that self-defense is not available if the defendant could reasonably have retreated from the threatened harm. Other jurisdictions do not require retreat. As with self-defense, defense of others allows a defendant can use reasonable force to protect a third party who reasonably appears to be under threat of imminent harm. Some jurisdictions require that the third party must have actually been under threat of imminent harm.

Defense of property allows a defendant to use reasonable force to prevent intrusion or dispossession of property. Before using reasonable force, a defendant must first ask the party to cease and desist from the interference with property. A defendant can never use deadly force in defense of property. In the case of personal property, a defendant can take reasonable steps to recapture the personal property only if the defendant acts timely after the dispossession with the personal property or after his discovery of the dispossession.

The necessity defense can be broken down into private necessity and public necessity. Under the defense of private necessity, a defendant has the right to interfere with a plaintiff's property in order to mitigate or avoid an imminent private harm or injury arising from a natural occurrence or some event unrelated to the plaintiff's use of the property. A defendant will have to pay plaintiff reasonable compensation for any harm that occurs to plaintiff's property from the defendant's interference. Under the defense of public necessity, a defendant, usually the state or a public official, has the right to interfere with plaintiff's property in order to avoid an imminent social injury. A defendant does not have to pay a plaintiff compensation for the harm to the property from the defendant's interference.

A FEW WORDS ABOUT REMEDIES

You should conclude your analysis of an intentional tort problem with an analysis of remedies. The general principles of compensatory and punitive damages, discussed in Chapter Eight, apply here as well. A plaintiff can obtain compensatory damages from a defendant to make the plaintiff whole. In general, compensatory damages for intentional torts include personal injury, damages to compensate for injury to property, and damages to compensate for the emotional harm and dignitary injuries associated with battery, assault, false imprisonment, or intentional infliction of emotional distress. Furthermore, if a defendant acted willfully, punitive damages are also available. See Chapter Eight for more details.

A FEW WORDS ABOUT NUISANCE

Your Torts class might cover the topic of Nuisance, a cause of action that is shared by Torts and Property. Nuisance is often compared with trespass to land because both deal with injuries to real property. Trespass is an intentional physical invasion of land. Nuisance, by contrast, entails an interference with the use of land. If someone stands right at the border of your property and repeatedly makes a loud, disturbing noise, that keeps you awake, there is no trespass to land (because there is no physical invasion), but there is a nuisance.

There are two types of nuisance claims: private nuisance and public nuisance. A private nuisance is an invasion of another's interest in the private use and enjoyment of land that is either (i) intentional and unreasonable or (ii) unintentional and arising out of negligent or reckless conduct or abnormally dangerous conditions or activities. An invasion is unreasonable under (i) if (a) the gravity of the harm outweighs the benefit of the defendant's conduct or (b) the harm caused by the conduct is serious and the financial burden of compensating for the harm would not make the defendant's activities feasible. The elements of private nuisance are complicated because they reflect generations of court decisions on what types of activities constitute a nuisance. Essentially, private nuisance involves activity by the defendant which affects how the plaintiff uses and enjoys private property. The court, under the elements of nuisance, has to determine whether the harm produced by the defendant's activities to the plaintiff outweighs the benefits. In determining the benefits, the court can consider the social utility, the suitability of the activity in the location where it is occurring, and the feasibility of moving or curtailing the activity.

A public nuisance is an unreasonable interference with a right common to the general public. An interference is unreasonable if it has a significant effect on public safety, peace, health, comfort or convenience or if the activity has a significant effect on a public right, that may be defined by statute. Often public nuisance claims are brought by a state official, such as a state attorney general. But a private citizen can bring a public nuisance claim if the private plaintiff can show harm to a private property interest.

■ **PROBLEMS** ■

1. Suppose Dudley is driving on a narrow one way street onto which a box has fallen. In order to avoid hitting the box, Dudley drives onto the sidewalk to get around the box and in so doing runs over Prentice's flowerbed, killing all the flowers. What are the arguments for and against the statement that Dudley acted with intent under these facts?

2.   Prentice and David were hiking in the mountains. While going through some rough terrain, Prentice was bitten in the leg by a snake and passed out from shock. David immediately called for emergency assistance on his cellular phone. While Prentice was unconscious, David, who is not a physician but was trained in first aid, applied a tourniquet to the wound and cut out a portion of Prentice's skin in order to be able to suck out the poison. When David finished applying the first aid, an emergency helicopter arrived to take Prentice to the local poison center, where he regained consciousness. Prentice was treated by a doctor who informed Prentice that the area around his wound had been badly damaged when David cut it and that he would need further treatment. Prentice told the doctor to do whatever was needed to make him better. The doctor proceeded to recut the area treated by David and applied several treatments in order to heal the wound. The treatments caused Prentice to feel an intense burning sensation in his leg and pass out. When Prentice awoke, he saw that his leg was wrapped in a tight, thick gauze and he was informed by the doctor that he had suffered muscle damage that would require further therapy after the wounds were completely healed. Analyze Prentice's claims for intentional torts against David and the doctor, including any defenses.

Suggested Answers

1.   Prentice versus Dudley:

Prentice can show intent in two ways. First, Prentice can establish that Dudley had the purpose to make the consequences of his actions occur. Alternatively, Prentice can establish that Dudley had the knowledge that the consequences would occur with substantial certainty. The consequences here would be the killing of the flowers. It would be hard for Prentice to establish that Dudley's purpose was to kill the flowers. Under these facts, it looks like Dudley's purpose was to avoid the box, but inadvertently ran over the flowers. The substantial certainty approach may have more promise. Under the second approach, Prentice would have to show that when Dudley acted, he knew that his acts would kill the flowers with substantial certainty, which means there was a high probability that the flowers would be killed when he drove over the sidewalk. Prentice would have to show that Dudley knew about the flowers and was aware about the direction in which his car was moving towards the flowers. If Prentice fails to show that Dudley was even aware of the flowers, intent may be difficult to show. But that does not rule out the possibility that Dudley was at fault; he did not act with ordinary care.

2.   Prentice versus David:

Prentice's claim will be for battery. The elements are arguably present under the majority approach. David did make physical contact with Prentice, and he acted in a way that showed a purpose or knowledge with substantial certainty that physical contact would be made with Prentice. The physical contact was offensive or harmful, which would be assessed under standards of reasonableness. Here, David did cut out part of Prentice's skin, and this would offend a reasonable sense of dignity as required for the prima facie case.

The heart of the problem is one of defenses. David would most likely raise the defense of consent. Here there is no express consent since Prentice had passed out, and it is unlikely that Prentice had provided consent for this type of invasion before they ventured out. Absent evidence of express consent, David would have to argue implied consent. David may argue that the situation is a medical emergency in which courts have found that consent is implied. The problem is that those cases involved doctors. David is not a doctor, but he did have first aid training and was acting like a doctor. He could make the argument that by analogy, he should be able to rely on the medical emergency cases. How the court decides will be based on how it views those cases. If they were meant to apply only to professional doctors, as a form of professional regulation, then the court may be reluctant to expand the defense. However, the court could view these cases as being about the patient and therefore make the analogy.

As an alternative, David could argue implied consent based upon the circumstances. When two people go out on hikes like these, the assumption is that they look out for each other. The implied assumption is that each will do what is necessary to help the other and avoid injury. If, for example, Prentice were about to be hit by a boulder and David pushed him out of the way (a battery), there would be a basis for consent given the circumstances. Arguably, this fact pattern is similar: David was administering first aid to alleviate the snake bite. From Prentice's perspective, the scope of this implied consent is quite broad. He would argue that he did not consent to have his leg hurt in the way that David did. But that argument is about how carefully or prudently David administered the first aid, which would be a negligence case.

Finally, David might try necessity. The problem is that necessity cases are largely about use of property, rather than invasion of the person. Nonetheless, the principle of lesser evil might apply as in private necessity. David's choice was between waiting for help and administering first aid as he did. He made the choice that involved less harm. The situation is different from the standard necessity case, however, which involves defendant using plaintiff's property to help himself. Here, David is invading Prentice's person to help Prentice. Given that David gets no benefit here and was seeking to help Prentice, that difference may weigh in favor of necessity, when understood in either moral or cost-benefit terms.

The last set of arguments may sound like a defense of third party argument. The problem is that David is not protecting a third party against Prentice or Prentice against a third party. Nonetheless, the defense of third party argument can be made. The majority rule is the judge the defense with a reasonableness standard as seen from the perspective of the third party being defended while the minority views it from the perspective of the defendant. Either way, it was arguably reasonable for David to administer first aid under these facts, but there is a question of whether he administered first aid in a reasonable manner. The last point would overlap with a breach analysis under negligence.

Prentice versus Doctor:

The doctor has several grounds for raising the consent defense here. The first is the emergency defense. The second is

Prentice's express consent. The analysis would rest on how one interprets Prentice's words: do everything you need to help me. This consent would allow the doctor to pursue a course of conduct that would attempt to improve Prentice's condition, and is obviously quite broad. If the doctor acted in a way that would be outside that course of conduct, then he would have exceeded Prentice's consent and the defense fails. Whether the doctor acted in a way that is consistent with treatment for improving Prentice's condition will depend upon how such injuries are treated, and we would need more facts about that. These facts invite a negligence analysis, and we will discuss that issue when we cover medical malpractice. The two big issues under negligence would be the standard of care by which to judge the doctor's conduct and the issue of informed consent: was Prentice warned of the relevant risks associated with the procedure.

CHECKLIST FOR INTENTIONAL TORTS ✓

A. Keep in mind three issues in analyzing intentional torts:

    1. The defendant must have acted with intent.

    2. The defendant's act must fall within one or more of the seven intentional torts.

    3. The defendant may have a defense which would make the defendant not liable for the tort.

B. Intent:

    1. General standard: to show that defendant acted with intent, plaintiff must show either:

        a. defendant acted with the purpose of producing the consequence of the act; or

        b. defendant acted with the knowledge that the consequence of the act would occur with substantial certainty.

    2. Special issue: dual intent. The general view is that the

defendant intended the act, not the consequences of the act. However, some jurisdictions require dual intent: the defendant must have intended both the act and the harm that was the consequence of the act.

C. The Seven Intentional Torts: Remember the elements and issues raised for each claim:

1. Battery: defendant intended to cause a harmful or offensive contact with the physical person of another and such contact either directly or indirectly occurred.

   a. Most jurisdictions require only that the defendant intended the contact not that the contact be harmful or offensive. However, in dual intent jurisdictions, the defendant must intend that there is contact and that the contact is harmful or offensive.

   b. Harm occurs if there is physical injury, even a relatively minor one.

   c. Offense occurs if the contact offends a reasonable sense of dignity.

2. Assault: defendant intended either (a) to cause a harmful or offensive contact with the person of another or (b) to cause immediate apprehension of a harmful or offensive contact and the plaintiff thereby is put in immediate apprehension of a harmful or offensive contact.

   a. If a defendant's conduct results in a harmful or offensive contact, the defendant is liable for battery only. An assault claim merges into a battery claim if a harmful or offensive contact occurs. If there is only an immediate apprehension of a harmful or offensive contact, but no actual contact, then the defendant is liable for an assault, not a battery.

   b. The apprehension by the plaintiff must be imminent. A conditional threat of future harm cannot be the basis for an assault claim.

3. False Imprisonment: defendant (1) intentionally confines

a plaintiff, (2) against the plaintiff's will, and (3) the plaintiff is aware of the confinement.

    a. Plaintiff must be completely confined with no reasonable means of escape. If the means of escape imposes a risk of harm to a plaintiff, the plaintiff's personal property, or to third parties, then confinement is complete.

4. Intentional infliction of emotional distress: defendant intentionally caused severe emotional distress in plaintiff by engaging in extreme and outrageous conduct.

    a. Extreme and outrageous conduct is determined by community standards, usually based on the average member of the community.

5. Trespass to land: defendant (a) intentionally enters, or causes a thing or a third party to enter, the land in possession of another, (b) intentionally remains on the land after permission to be on the land is removed, or (c) intentionally fails to remove from the land an item that the defendant is obligated to remove.

    a. Plaintiff does not have to show any harm to the land or to the person to recover for trespass to land. The injury is in the violation of the plaintiff's right to exclusive possession of the land.

6. Trespass to chattels: defendant (a) intentionally dispossessed another person of personal property or (b) intentionally used or intermeddled through physical contact with the personal property in possession of another.

    a. Unlike trespass to land, trespass to chattels requires the plaintiff to show actual harm that resulted from the trespass to personal property. This actual harm can include loss of use for a significant period of time, harm to the plaintiff's person or personal property, or damage to the condition of the personal property.

7. Conversion: defendant intentionally exercised dominion

or control over the personal property of plaintiff so as to seriously interfere with the right of the plaintiff to control the personal property.

    a.   A plaintiff need not show actual harm to recover under conversion.

    b.   Conversion and trespass to chattels both cover intentional torts against personal property. Conversion covers interference with the plaintiff's rights of ownership and control over the personal property. Trespass to chattels covers interference with a plaintiff's rights of possession over the personal property.

D. Defenses: a defendant can raise several defenses against plaintiff's claim of an intentional tort. These defenses apply to all the intentional torts. Remember that a defendant has the burden to raise and prove these defenses.

    1.   Consent: plaintiff agreed to defendant's conduct that resulted in the intentional tort. The agreement can be express (such as through a contract) or implied through the conduct of the plaintiff.

        a.   Consent has boundaries, and if a defendant's conduct goes beyond these boundaries, then consent does not apply. The scope of consent depends on the facts and circumstances of the case and the standards of society for the behavior at issue.

        b.   A plaintiff's consent must be informed. If consent is obtained by trickery or force, then the defense does not apply. The amount of information necessary is based on what a reasonable person would need to know in order to agree to defendant's conduct.

        c.   A defendant can raise defense of consent if a reasonable person would have believed that the plaintiff had consented and the defendant in fact did believe that the plaintiff had consented.

    2.   Defense of self: defendant can use reasonable force if the

defendant reasonably believes that a plaintiff is about to commit harmful conduct on the defendant. The threatened conduct can be any type of tort, intentional, negligent, or strict liability.

    a. For force to be reasonable, it must not be disproportionate to the threatened harm. Deadly force is reasonable only if the threat reasonably appears to be deadly or of serious bodily harm.

    b. Courts are split on whether a defendant is required to retreat. Some jurisdictions hold that self-defense is not available if a defendant could reasonably have retreated from the threatened harm. Other jurisdictions do not require retreat.

3. Defense of third parties: as with self-defense, defendant can use reasonable use to protect a third party who reasonable appears to be in imminent harm. Some jurisdictions require that the third party must have actually been subjected to imminent harm.

4. Defense of property: defendant can use reasonable force to prevent intrusion or dispossession of property. Before using reasonable force, a defendant must first ask a party to cease and desist from the interference with property. A defendant can never use deadly force in defense of property.

    a. In the case of personal property, defendant can take reasonable steps to recapture the personal property only if the defendant acts timely after the dispossession with the personal property or after his discovery of the dispossession.

5. Defense of private necessity: defendant has the right to interfere with a plaintiff's property in order to mitigate or avoid an imminent private harm or injury arising from a natural occurrence or some event unrelated to the plaintiff's use of the property.

    a. A defendant will have to pay a plaintiff reasonable compensation for any harm that occurs to plaintiff's property from the defendant's interference.

    6. Defense of public necessity: defendant, usually the state or a public official, has the right to interfere with plaintiff's property in order to avoid an imminent social injury.

        a. A defendant does not have to pay a plaintiff compensation for the harm to the property from defendant's interference.

E. Remedies: if a defendant is found liable for an intentional tort, the defendant must compensate a plaintiff for the injury and may be liable for punitive damages. See Chapter Eight for more details.

F. Nuisance: consists of two separate legal claims, a private nuisance or a public nuisance.

    1. Private nuisance: an invasion of a private use and enjoyment of land that is

        a. EITHER intentional and unreasonable, where an invasion is unreasonable if

            (i) the gravity of the harm outweighs the benefit of the defendant's conduct, or

            (ii) the harm caused by the conduct is serious and the financial burden of compensating for the harm would not make the defendant's activities feasible;

        b. OR unintentional and arising out of negligent or reckless conduct or abnormally dangerous conditions or activities.

    2. Public nuisance: unreasonable interference with a right common to the general public. An interference is unreasonable if it has a significant effect on public safety, peace, health, comfort or convenience or if the activity has a significant effect on a public right, that may be defined by statute.

CHAPTER 3

Negligence: Duty of Care

GENERAL APPROACH

In most Torts classes, the negligence cause of action will take up most of the class. In United States Torts law, negligence has been the primary claim that arises in litigation, and the reasonableness standard is pervasive in the law. The reason for the emphasis on negligence is that it's a flexible cause of action, allowing many legal claims to be brought under its broad standard. As a result, there is a lot of case law on negligence, and the subject is a broad one. This book, like your course, divides up negligence into its pieces. We will talk very briefly about how the pieces fit together.

In order to establish a claim of negligence against a defendant, a plaintiff has to show four elements: duty, breach, causation, and damages. Under the duty element, the plaintiff must show that the defendant owed a duty of reasonable care to the plaintiff. This element is the focus of this chapter. To satisfy the breach element, the plaintiff must show that the defendant's conduct fell below the standard of reasonableness. This element is the subject of the next chapter. To establish causation, the plaintiff must show that the defendant's unreasonable conduct caused injury to the plaintiff. This element is the subject of Chapter Five. Finally, the plaintiff must show that the injury suffered constitutes recoverable damages under the law. Injury is the subject of Chapter Six. Finally, the defendant might have several defenses to the claim of negligence.

These defenses are presented in Chapter Nine because they overlap with the defenses that arise under claims for strict liability that are also discussed in that chapter.

GENERAL DUTY OF REASONABLE CARE

Under the law of negligence, a defendant owes a duty towards others to act reasonably. Given the broad scope of the duty under the law, it's not difficult for the plaintiff to establish the element of duty for a negligence claim. However, there are special duty rules that you need to be aware of and consider as you analyze a negligence problem. There are also some general issues that you need to be aware of in order to avoid confusion during your reading and your class discussion.

First, duty is a legal question for a judge to determine. It does not rest upon factual determinations that are particular to a case. Instead, the duty element establishes a broad standard that applies to all cases. As a result, the duty element is the most rule-like of all the four elements of negligence. Unlike breach, causation, and damages, each of which will depend on the facts of a particular case, the duty element is not based on the facts of a case. Once a judge has determined that a defendant does not owe a duty to a plaintiff the judge has created a rule that applies to all negligence cases, regardless of the facts of the case.

Second, and related to the first point, the duty element often becomes confused with the causation element of negligence, specifically the proximate cause prong of causation. We discuss this point again in Chapter Six under causation, but the point is also worth highlighting now. In your Torts class, you might hear that the duty element is based on foreseeability—specifically that a defendant's duty extends to foreseeable victims or foreseeable harms. Technically, this statement confuses the duty element with the causation element. Under the causation element, the defendant is liable for foreseeable harms to foreseeable victims. Whether a victim or a harm is foreseeable is a question of the facts of a particular case as well as the law. So, foreseeability is an element of causation, rather than of the general duty of care. But once foreseeability is determined in a particular case, the court establishes a rule applicable to other cases.

Remember that under the law of negligence, a defendant owes a duty to act reasonably to everyone. The duty element is a matter for a judge and is based on a legal rule, rather than the facts of a particular case. The foreseeability of a harm or of a victim is important in determining the element of proximate cause. Once foreseeability is determined in a particular case, however, a rule is established that may be applied to other cases. The special duty issues that are highlighted below illustrate how duty rules are created.

SPECIAL DUTY ISSUES

The law of negligence has established special duty rules. These rules sometimes determine that a defendant does not have a duty to a plaintiff. In other cases, the special duty rules determine the scope of the duty that the defendant owes to the plaintiff. In understanding these special duty rules, keep in mind the circumstances to which these rules apply and how they apply.

Nonfeasance or Omission

The most famous special duty rule under the law of negligence is the "no duty to rescue" rule. Under this rule, a defendant does not have a duty to rescue a plaintiff who is in distress. Sometimes the rule is stated in terms of there being no duty to act. You may also hear the rule phrased in terms of no tort liability for nonfeasance or omissions by the defendant. You will also encounter many policy arguments for and against the rule. The argument against the rule rests on its harshness. If a defendant could have helped a plaintiff with minimal effort, why shouldn't the defendant be liable to the plaintiff for negligence? More urgently, critics of the rule point to the selfishness and lack of civility implied by the rule. Defenders of the rule point to broad concepts of individual responsibility, self-help, and protection of individual autonomy in deciding whom to help and whom not to help. More practically, defenders of the rule point to practical questions of administration.

After all, there is always someone in distress somewhere. If there was an affirmative duty to rescue, everyone would always be in breach because it's not feasible to help everyone at all times. Therefore, the blanket rule of no duty is a practical rule to limit tort liability.

In terms of your practical understanding of this special duty rule, keep in mind that a defendant does not owe a duty to rescue a plaintiff. So if the plaintiff's claim rests on the defendant's failure to act, then the plaintiff will have a difficult time establishing the duty element of negligence. But there are some exceptions to this rule.

First, some jurisdictions have enacted a statute that establishes a duty to rescue. Failure to rescue might give rise to a statutory violation with the resulting fines and penalties. If such a statute applies, your professor will let you know about it. Keep in mind that most jurisdictions have also enacted a Good Samaritan statute, which limits the liability of someone who does affirmatively attempt to rescue a plaintiff but harms the plaintiff in the process. Such statutes often apply to individuals who are specially trained in rescue techniques such as medical professionals or firemen.

Second, a defendant does have a duty to rescue if a plaintiff is injured as part of an undertaking by the defendant. Suppose the defendant has created a risky situation, such as an automobile accident, and the plaintiff is injured by debris in the road from the accident left by the defendant. The defendant cannot argue that there was no duty to rescue the plaintiff if the defendant created the hazard. This exception is often summarized by the phrase "danger invites rescue."

Special Relationships

There are also several special relationships which impose a duty to act on a defendant. Remember these special rules as (1) custodial relationships; (2) landowner duties; and (3) duties to control third parties.

Custodial relationships. If a plaintiff is in the custody of a defendant, then there is duty on the part of the defendant to rescue the plaintiff. A custodial relationship can be created through law, such as a familial relationship or a guardianship, or through circumstances. Suppose a plaintiff is out with a defendant and the plaintiff becomes inebriated. The defendant takes the plaintiff home in his car, but leaves him in the car overnight to become sober. The plaintiff is in a custodial relationship with the defendant, and the defendant will owe a duty towards the plaintiff. If the plaintiff is injured while left in the car, then the plaintiff can establish the element of duty in a negligence claim against the defendant.

Duties of a landowner. A landowner owes special duties to those who come onto the land. The duty owed depends upon the reason for being on the land. These rules are often fairly detailed and complicated, but can be broken down as follows.

If a plaintiff is a trespasser—someone who comes onto land without the permission of a landowner—the landowner has a duty to not intentionally injure the plaintiff. In general, if a trespasser is injured because of a landowner's unreasonable conduct, the tres-passer cannot establish the duty element, and does not have a claim for negligence. You will see the issue of "active operations" arise in this context. If a landowner has an active operation, such as a factory or machinery, then the landowner owes a duty to a trespasser to prevent harm from the operation of the factory or machinery.

If a plaintiff is a licensee, then a landowner has the duty to warn of known hazards on the land and to keep the land reason-ably safe from known hazards. A licensee is someone who comes onto land with the permission of a landowner and for the purpose of the licensee. An example is a social guest who comes onto the land for the purpose of entertainment at the landowner's home.

If a plaintiff is an invitee, then a landowner has a general duty of care to the plaintiff. An invitee is someone who comes onto land with the permission of a landowner and for the purpose of the landowner. An example is a business customer who comes into a retail establishment to shop.

Landowner duties can be complicated, but do not become overwhelmed by the rules. In approaching a question that raises landowner duties, keep in mind the different categories of plaintiffs based on whether they have permission to come onto the land and what their purpose is for entering a landowner's property. Also keep in mind that some courts have changed these rules by imposing a general duty of care owed by a landowner to an invitee and a licensee with a lesser duty owed to a trespasser.

Duty to control third parties. There are several situations in which a defendant has a duty to control the actions of third parties over which the defendant exercises control or authority. Failure to take reasonable steps to control a third party can be the basis for liability under negligence to a plaintiff injured by the third party. One situation where such a duty arises is in the parent-child relationship. Parents have a duty to control the actions of their children. An employer has a duty to control the actions of an employee. Notice that this duty allows a plaintiff to bring a negligence suit against both a third party and a party who failed to exercise control. Sometimes suing both parties might be appropriate. Sometimes a plaintiff may choose to go after only one of two parties, perhaps a party who failed to exercise control, since this party may have deeper pockets. The question of whom to sue is a matter of litigation strategy and a question of the law of civil procedure. Under tort law, however, a duty exists on a party who could have exercised control or authority to prevent a third party from causing harm.

In Chapter Ten, we discuss a topic called "vicarious liability" which you should not confuse with the duty to control third parties. Under the doctrine of vicarious liability, a person is also liable for the actions of a third party, but the liability does not extend from a breach of duty, but from a special legal relationship between the person who is vicariously liable and the third party. One example of vicarious liability is the doctrine of respondeat superior—the liability of the employer for the torts of an employee. Under the doctrine of respondeat superior, an employer is liable if an employee is held liable for conduct that occurs in the course of employment. The difference between vicarious liability and a duty to control third parties (like an employee) is that, under the doctrine of respondeat superior, a plaintiff has to show only that the third party (such as an employee) is negligent. The liability of the employer arises automatically once the liability of the employee has been established. Under a duty to control third parties, however, a plaintiff has to show that a third party is liable and that a party who had a duty to control failed to exercise reasonable control over the third party. The two legal claims are different and should be understood separately.

We discuss vicarious liability in Chapter Ten in more detail, but here are some examples to help you understand the concepts discussed in the previous paragraph. Suppose an employee has acted unreasonably towards a co-worker. The co-worker may have a claim of negligence against the employee. The co-worker can also bring a claim of negligence against the employer for failure to exercise his duty to control the employee. Furthermore, if the employee's unreasonable conduct was in the course of employment, then the employer would be vicariously liable if the co-worker can establish the employee's liability.

Now take another example. Suppose an older child is put in charge of a younger sibling. The sibling does something unreasonable that hurts a plaintiff. The plaintiff can bring a claim against the sibling and against the older child. The claim against the older child would be based on a duty to control third parties. But the plaintiff in this case would not have a claim against the older child on a theory of vicarious liability since there is no relationship of employer-employee between the older child and his sibling.

Another situation where vicarious liability does not apply is in the psychiatrist-patient relationship. But some courts have found a duty on the part of a psychiatrist to control a patient who poses a harm to a foreseeable person. In the famous case of *Tarasoff v. Board of Regents of California*, 551 P.2d 334 (Cal. 1976), a patient informed a university psychiatrist of intentions to harm a female student on campus. The student was killed by the patient. The psychiatrist did take steps to warn the victim and prevent the crime. The court ruled that there was a legal duty to control the patient and take reasonable steps to warn the foreseeable victim. Many states have imposed such a duty on mental health care professionals.

Public Policy

Courts will decline to impose a duty when public policy is implicated. This limitation on duty arises when a governmental entity, such as a public utility or a police force, is being sued. For example, if there is a power failure resulting from an act by the public utility and someone is injured, the injured party does not have a claim against the utility. The reasoning is that the entity owed a duty to the public at large and not to any particular member of the public. The same reasoning applies to suits against a police force for failure to aid a victim of crime. Unless special circumstances, such as a custodial relationship, warrant the imposition of a duty, courts are hesitant to impose one.

There are two points to keep in mind about the public policy limitation on duty. First, this limitation is different from the defense of sovereign immunity, under which a private citizen cannot sue a governmental entity or the state. All states have waived sovereign immunity to a certain extent, but even if there is a waiver, courts will find a public policy limitation of duty. There are two policy reasons for this limitation. The first is a practical one. If the state or a governmental entity were liable for all harms to the public, then the extent of liability could be quite great and the state's resources would be overly burdened. As a result, the public policy limitation serves to put some caps on liability. The second policy reason is a about false litigation. If someone is injured during a power outage, for example, it may not be possible to know with certainty whether the injury was the result of the power outage, the carelessness of the victim, or the actions of some third party. Consequently, courts have avoided imposing liability for public policy reasons if the extent of liability would be too great or create the possibility of false claims.

The second point to keep in mind concerns when courts do impose a duty on a governmental entity like a public utility or a police force—the exception to the limitation. If a plaintiff is in a custodial relationship with a governmental agent (like a police officer) and relies on this relationship, then some courts will impose a duty. Such a custodial relationship may be difficult to show, but one example of such a relationship in which reliance can be shown is the creation of a 911 or emergency call service which people can use to call for assistance in the event of a crisis. A failure of such a service that results in injury to a plaintiff can be the basis for imposing a duty on the state or governmental entity that promoted the service and created the reliance.

Emotional Harm

If a plaintiff is physically injured by a defendant, then the plaintiff can recover damages for emotional harm, known as "pain and suffering." In general, if a plaintiff isn't physically injured, but merely witnesses a defendant causing harm (perhaps hitting someone or running into them with a car), then the plaintiff cannot recover for the emotional harm suffered. The exception to this rule is that a plaintiff can recover for emotional harm caused by being in the "zone of danger" and witnessing a close relative being physically injured by a defendant. By "zone of danger," we mean that a plaintiff was in the physical range of being hurt by a defendant, but was not in fact physically injured. A close relative means a parent, a child or a sibling, although some courts have extended the definition to include more distant relatives. Some courts also require that a plaintiff is an eyewitness to the accident. For these courts, a plaintiff that merely hears the accident occur or sees it on videotape cannot recover.

Economic Harm

If a plaintiff is physically injured by a defendant, then the plaintiff can recover economic damages such as lost wages or medical expenses. However, if a plaintiff is not physically injured but suffers economic harm as a result of a defendant's negligence, the plaintiff cannot recover from the defendant. This rule is stated as a defendant having no duty to prevent economic harm absent physical impact—the physical impact rule. For example, suppose a defendant negligently runs into a car moving in front of him on the highway. The driver of the struck car will have a negligence claim against the defendant. But drivers that are caught in traffic behind the accident who suffer delay that results in economic harm will have no claim against the defendant since they suffered no physical impact.

The exception to this rule of no duty for economic harm is liability for professionals like accountants and attorneys. If an accountant or attorney act negligently in working for a client and the negligence results in economic loss, then the injured client can recover the economic loss. Suppose an accountant negligently reviews a company's accounts and states that the company is solvent when it is not. A creditor relying on the accountant's audit lends the company money which is lost. The accountant can be liable for the economic loss from the loan. Similarly, if an attorney negligently drafts a will for a client and the will turns out to be invalid, then heirs of the client who are disinherited as a result would have a claim for the economic loss against the attorney. Notice in each of these cases the negligence resulted in pure economic loss, but given the policy of protecting the public from professionals that handle business and finance, a duty to prevent economic loss is imposed on defendants in these cases.

One final thought to keep in mind: just because a duty exists doesn't mean that the defendant is automatically liable. Duty is only one of four elements a plaintiff has to establish for a defendant to be liable. Remember that all four elements are duty, breach, causation, and damages.

■ PROBLEMS ■

---

1.   Defendant runs a day care center that includes an indoor play and recreation room and an outdoor playground that includes a swing set and a slide. The center is licensed by the state and complies with all applicable regulations. One day A and B, both five years old, are playing on the swing set when a stray dog enters the playground and bites B before running away. The playground is open and not fenced in. Several other children (all the way from C to Z) have been bitten by a stray dog in the playground before. Defendant cleans B's wound and places a bandage over the bite,

but does not take B to the hospital. Instead, when B's parent picks up B at the end of the day, Defendant informs B's parent about the incident. B is immediately taken to the hospital where he is examined. The doctor finds that there is some chance of rabies and gives B a series of shots to deal with the potential disease. B's parent has to pay $4000 in hospital bills and has to miss three days of work to take care of B. In addition, B has developed a fear of the family dog, who must be given away, and B develops emotional distress at the thought of the bite and the shots, which manifests itself in loss of sleep and occasional and unexpected nausea. B's parent and B sue Defendant for negligence, claiming that Defendant's unreasonable conduct resulted in the dog bite, the hospital expenses, and B's trauma. Analyze the arguments for and against Defendant's duty as part of the negligence claim.

Suggested Answers

1. Plaintiffs need to establish that Defendant owed them a duty of care in order to establish a negligence claim. Defendant most likely will try to argue that Plaintiff cannot establish the element of duty because Defendant did not do anything affirmative that would have created a duty. Furthermore, Defendant may argue that there was no special relationship that would have created a duty to act. Plaintiff, however, has arguments to establish the prima facie case for duty.

Plaintiffs have an argument based on foreseeability. Here, several facts support Plaintiffs' argument for duty based on foreseeability. Several other children have been bitten in a way similar to the accident in this case. Here, 24 other children have been attacked and that history should weigh in favor of Plaintiffs. Here, the facts that the property was not fenced in and used specifically by children also weigh in favor of Plaintiffs, especially given the history of dog bite incidents.

In addition, someone who volunteers to rescue a person has a duty to prevent foreseeable injury. Here, even if Defendant would not be liable for the dogbite, Defendant did begin to take care of

Plaintiff by administering first aid. Defendant, however, failed to take Plaintiff to the hospital in time. Plaintiff has an argument that hospital care was foreseeable in light of the injuries and that would be the basis for imposing a duty on Defendant. Furthermore, Defendant was acting as a parent since he was providing day care services. Therefore, an argument exist under that statement of the common law trends to impose a duty here.

The duty of landowners would be relevant here as well. In this case, B is most likely an invitee, someone who has come on the land for the purposes of a landowner. Put another way, customers of a business establishment are considered invitees, and B here is a customer. Landowners owe invitees the highest duty of care to protect against unreasonable dangers on the land. The difficulty here is that the danger (the dog) entered onto the land and is arguably not a dangerous condition of the land. Plaintiff does have an argument, however, that the land being unfenced and being used as a playground is a dangerous condition which the land-owner had to duty to remedy. There is also an argument that the children in the playground are licensees rather than invitees and so a lower duty was owed to them.

Note that the landowner duty argument would help with Plaintiff's claim for the dog bite. Since landowner would also have a duty to rescue, once an accident occurred due to a breach of a duty, the breach of the duty with respect to protecting the children from a dog bite would support a duty with respect to remedying the dog bite.

Finally, the question does not distinguish between the claims of B and the claims of her parents. However, any duty owed to the child would support a duty owed to the parents since the injuries claimed by the parent are derivative from he injuries suffered by the child. Furthermore, the parents did entrust the child with the day care center and that would support an independent basis for a duty under negligence based either on contract or on the special relationship of trust.

CHECKLIST FOR NEGLIGENCE: DUTY OF CARE

A. Elements of Negligence Claim: A plaintiff must establish duty, breach, causation, and damages. Keep these four elements in mind as you work through Chapters Three through Six.

B. The Duty of Care element: General duty

    1. Under negligence, there is a general duty to act in a reasonable manner. From this perspective, duty is an easy element to establish—but keep in mind the special cases that are laid out below.

    2. The duty element is a question of law, which means that a judge ultimately determines whether a defendant owed a duty to a plaintiff. The duty question does not depend on factual issues to be determined by a jury.

C. Special Duty Issues

    1. Nonfeasance or Omission: A defendant does not have a duty to rescue another person. In general, failure to rescue someone does not give rise to liability under negligence or Tort law more generally.

        a. Exception to no duty to rescue rule: If a defendant undertook a course of conduct that placed a plaintiff in danger, then the defendant owes the plaintiff a duty of care to rescue the plaintiff. Remember: "danger invites rescue."

    2. Special relationship: If a defendant is in a special relationship with a plaintiff, then is the defendant has a duty to act.

        a. Custodial relationship is an example of a special relationship: Suppose a defendant has been hired to take care of a plaintiff, such as a bodyguard or caregiver. Under these custodial situations, the defendant owes the plaintiff a duty of care to take reasonable steps to protect the plaintiff. Note that this relationship may be voluntary on the part of the defendant or imposed by law on the defendant (such as through a guardianship).

b. Landowners owe special duties to those who come onto the land and are injured. Some jurisdictions have created a general duty of care that a landowner owes to anyone who comes lawfully onto the land. Most jurisdictions define the duty based on the reason the person came onto the land.

  (i) Duty to trespassers: No duty is owed to a trespasser except not to intentionally injure the trespasser.

  (ii) Duty to invitee: A general duty of care is owed to an invitee—someone who comes onto the land by invitation of a landowner for the landowner's business.

  (iii) Duty to licensee: A duty to warn of known defects and keep the property reasonably safe of known hazards is owed to a licensee, who is someone who comes onto the land with the limited permission of a landowner for some purpose other than the landowner's business.

c. If a defendant has control over a third party, then there is a duty to take care that the third party does not harm other parties. An example of this situation would be a parent's obligation to control a child or an employer's obligation to control an employee in the workplace.

  (i) *Tarasoff* duties: A psychiatrist has a duty towards a foreseeable plaintiff who may be harmed by the psychiatrist's patient.

3. Public Policy: There can be limits on the duty of care owed by public utilities and governmental entities to

individual plaintiffs. In general, there is no duty of care owed to a particular plaintiff by a public utility or a governmental entity if the entity does not take reasonable steps to protect the public. Legal liability in these situations is limited to obligations owed under contract and to intentional tort claims.

4. Emotional harm: In general, a defendant does not owe a duty for emotional harm that a bystander suffers when he witnesses a tort committed by the defendant. The exception is if a bystander is in the zone of danger created by a defendant's conduct and witnesses a close relative injured by the defendant. To be in the "zone of danger," the bystander must have almost been physically injured by the defendant. A close relative includes a parent, a sibling, or an offspring.

5. Economic harm: In general, a defendant does not owe a duty for economic harm suffered by a plaintiff unless the economic harm comes from a physical impact to the plaintiff's property or person. An exception to this rule is the duty owed by an accountant or attorney for professional malpractice that arises from professional malpractice.

CHAPTER 4

Negligence: Breach Through Unreasonable Conduct

GENERAL APPROACH

The second element of a plaintiff's claim for negligence is breach of duty through unreasonable conduct. The element of breach is established by showing that a defendant failed to act like a reasonable person would have acted under the circumstances. The standard of reasonableness is meant to be open-ended and flexible, depending on the circumstances and the facts of a particular case. Many students and practicing attorneys find the reasonableness standard frustrating because it is unpredictable and so open-ended. But these characteristics are precisely what makes the reasonableness standard desirable from a broader policy perspective. Instead of dictating at the outset when a defendant will or will not be liable, the law is allowed to develop based on the circumstances and evolving attitudes about what conduct is or is not acceptable.

The reasonableness standard allows liability to be determined in a flexible manner, depending on the particular context of a case. Flexible, however, does not mean completely open-ended. There are certain defined and predictable ways in which attorneys have argued for the unreasonableness or reasonableness of a defendant's conduct. Even though the outcome of a specific case may not be completely known, the method through which reasonableness is argued and determined by attorneys is well-established and well-defined. This chapter will present these established arguments after a brief discussion of the role of judge and jury in determining when the defendant has acted unreasonably.

JUDGE VERSUS JURY

A plaintiff has a burden to show all four elements of the claim for negligence. This burden is established through a preponderance of the evidence, which means that in order to prevail, a plaintiff's evidence has to be slightly stronger than a defendant's. One question is whether a judge can decide, based on the evidence presented, whether a defendant was unreasonable or whether a case has to go to a jury. In general, the question of whether a defendant's conduct is unreasonable is a question for a jury. Historically, the reasonableness standard was developed so a defendant could be judged by members of the community who would decide, based on the evidence, whether the defendant fell below the standard of care. In the famous case of *Vaughan v. Menlove*, 132 E.R. 490 (1837), the English common law case often viewed as establishing the reasonableness standard in tort law, the court stated that a reasonable person is a person of ordinary prudence within a community, and that it's up to members of this community, as represented through a jury, to determine whether a defendant should be liable. In *Vaughan v. Menlove*, the issue was whether the defendant had been unreasonable in maintaining a haystack which had caught on fire. The fire had spread and damaged the plaintiff's property. The issue of reasonableness was based on the standard of ordinary prudence as applied by the jury who would have a better sense of the practical details of haystack management than the judge.

But a judge can take the issue of reasonableness away from a jury. Sometimes a judge may be just as knowledgeable and just as good a representative of the community as a jury. Furthermore, a judge may have had experience with the facts of a particular case so that the judge can recognize whether a particular defendant has acted unreasonably. In such cases, a jury trial might not add very much to the determination of the case except expense and time. When a judge determines whether a defendant has acted unreasonably, however, the judge's determination can be a precedent for future cases. A jury's determination in answering a question of fact does not make a legal determination that binds future courts about what is or is not reasonable. A judge's decision, on the other hand, does establish a legal rule that can be applied in future cases. Consequently, some judges are hesitant to take the issue of reasonableness away from a jury because the judge's decision will bind future courts and takes away the flexibility that is a desirable feature of the reasonableness standard. As a result, in most instances, the issue of reasonableness tends to be a jury question. But keep in mind that in some situations where the value of jury deliberation might be minimal, a judge might answer the question of reasonableness based on the evidence presented without the aid of a jury.

WHAT TO CONSIDER IN DETERMINING REASONABLENESS

It is up to a plaintiff and a defendant in a particular case to present the relevant arguments. The plaintiff will introduce evidence that shows the defendant was unreasonable while the defendant will introduce evidence that the conduct was reasonable. A jury (or judge in some instances) will consider the evidence, and if the strength of the evidence is in favor of the plaintiff, then the plaintiff will have satisfied the second element of a negligence claim. As mentioned above, the reasonableness standard was designed to be flexible and open-ended, leaving the issue of reasonableness up to the creativity of plaintiffs and defendants to develop arguments about reasonableness. But the law of negligence has developed to include five types of arguments that typically provide the basis for determining whether conduct is reasonable or not. These five typical arguments involve: custom, the Hand Formula, statutes, *res ipsa loquitur*, and special categories of reasonable people. Make sure you work through each of these when you are posed with the issue of reasonableness.

Custom

What is typically done in certain situations can be evidence of reasonable conduct. In the famous case of *Vaughan v. Menlove*, the defendant was accused of not maintaining his haystack properly, resulting in a fire that damaged the plaintiff's property. In determining whether the defendant had acted reasonably, the court looked to how haystacks were typically maintained by people in the community and what the common knowledge of haystack maintenance was at the time. In more modern situations, custom as to driving, maintenance of one's land, maintenance of one's automobile and other personal property, and conduct in different social or business contexts can be evidence of what society deems a reasonable standard of conduct. Similarly, a defendant can also introduce evidence of custom to establish that the standard of reasonableness was not breached. In products liability cases, the industry standard for manufacturing or designing products can be evidence of reasonableness in determining whether there was a manufacturing or design defect. The use of custom is consistent with the notion that reasonableness is a question for the jury to decide with the judge deciding the issue of reasonableness in rare situations. The jury represents the community and its knowledge of customs.

Keep in mind that while custom is evidence of reasonableness, it's rarely conclusive as to whether specific conduct is reasonable or unreasonable. Just because a defendant acted contrary to custom does not mean the defendant was unreasonable as a matter of law. Similarly, just because a defendant complied with custom does not mean that the defendant was reasonable and therefore not liable. The custom itself may or may not have been reasonable. One big issue is that there is never complete uniformity as to what a particular custom is. Members of a community may disagree as to whether any conduct is customary, and in most situations, many different types of conduct are considered reasonable. Given this wide freedom to operate, evidence of custom can be introduced but will rarely determine the outcome of a case. Most often, a plaintiff and a defendant will introduce independent evidence of custom, and it is up to a jury to decide what, in fact, is customary and whether the custom itself is reasonable to uphold. Evidence of custom can include testimony from individuals who are familiar with a practice, including experts if the practice is something highly technical and specialized.

The one exception to the rule that custom is not conclusive evidence of reasonableness is in the field of medical malpractice. If a plaintiff is arguing that a medical professional—generally a hospital, nurse, doctor, or technician—fell below the standard of reasonableness, the plaintiff must bring in evidence of what the medical profession considers reasonable conduct under such circumstances. This evidence involves testimony from an expert about what the profession deems as customary conduct. Similarly, a defendant will bring in supporting evidence from an expert about what is customary conduct within the profession. In medical malpractice cases, the issue of what is customary is a key question and is often a matter of sorting through expert testimony on both sides. Once a custom has been identified, however, the custom is the standard for reasonableness. In a medical malpractice case, failure to comply with custom means that a defendant is unreasonable and so has breached the duty of care. Similarly, compliance with custom in a medical malpractice case means that a defendant was reasonable and hence has not breached the duty of care. Custom is conclusive evidence of breach in a medical malpractice case once the custom has been established.

The Hand Formula (BpL Analysis)

Another way to establish reasonableness is the Hand Formula, associated with Judge Learned Hand from his decision in *United States v. Carroll Towing Co.*, 159 F.2d 169 (2nd. Cir. 1947). This approach is the most famous and common way to address the issue of reasonableness. Even though it is phrased as a formula, it is not a mathematical test. The Hand Formula provides a guideline, or heuristic, to determine whether a particular conduct is reasonable or unreasonable.

Put simply, the Hand Formula entails comparing the costs and the benefits of undertaking a particular conduct. Suppose a plaintiff argues that a defendant was unreasonable for not hiring a security guard to prevent crime in an apartment building. The

Hand Formula would require the plaintiff to compare a burden (B), or cost, of hiring the security guard with the likely harm that would arise from not hiring the security guard. The likely harm includes the probability of harm occurring (p) and the extent of harm (L). If the burden is greater than the likely harm, then not hiring the security guard is reasonable conduct. If the burden is lower than the likely harm, then hiring the security guard is reasonable conduct. The Hand Formula is considered an attractive approach to addressing the issue of reasonableness because it's flexible and can cover a wide range of situations, including ones in which there may not be a clear custom or a governing statute.

It's important to remember that the Hand Formula isn't a numerical calculation. The formula is meant to guide conduct in an intuitive and flexible way. The formula also focuses attention on what is relevant for determining whether a particular conduct is reasonable or not: costs and the likelihood of harm. For these reasons, the Hand Formula is often seen as the heart of reasonableness analysis and a helpful tool to structure and analyze legal arguments. The formula, however, has been criticized for reducing legal liability to a matter of costs and benefits while ignoring legal rights. In the case of the security guard, for example, the Hand Formula ignores any rights to be safe in one's home as protected under the law. If it is not cost-effective to provide security, the formula would imply no liability for failure to provide security. In defense of the formula, tort law is itself a very practical enterprise for determining when a defendant should compensate a plaintiff for harm that the plaintiff has suffered. The Hand Formula provides a very practical way of answering that question of compensation.

Statutes and Negligence Per Se

Sometimes a statute might govern a particular conduct. Statutes against speeding, requiring the maintenance of land or personal property, and requiring security are all examples of relevant statutory law that may set a standard for reasonableness. Under the doctrine of negligence per se, violation of a statute is conclusive evidence of breach. Notice that the opposite is not true under the doctrine—compliance with a statute is not conclusive evidence of reasonableness.

Negligence per se applies in very specific circumstances. First, there must be a statute that applies to the conduct at issue in a particular case. The statute can be a criminal statute, a civil statute, a regulation, or an administrative rule. Violation of a relevant statute is negligence per se if the statute satisfies three criteria: (i) the harm a plaintiff suffered is a type of harm the statute was meant to prevent; (ii) the plaintiff is in a class of victims the statute was meant to protect; and (iii) the statute establishes a standard of conduct—tells people what to do or not do. A plaintiff must establish each of these three elements in order to establish negligence per se. If one of these three is not satisfied, then negligence per se does not apply.

Res Ipsa Loquitur (RIL)

In rare instances, an accident occurs in which any possible evidence of unreasonable conduct is destroyed or is impossible to retrieve. For example, a plane crash might result in all evidence of pilot error or mechanical failure being destroyed. As another example, a medical procedure might occur when the patient is under anesthesia and there are no witnesses, other than potential defendants, to any unreasonable conduct. In such unusual situations, courts have developed an approach to breach called "*res ipsa loquitur*," which means "the matter speaks for itself." Under *res ipsa loquitur*, the very fact that an accident has occurred is evidence of breach. *Res ipsa loquitur* is rarely conclusive evidence of breach. The doctrine allows a plaintiff to point to an accident itself as evidence of breach and survive motions to dismiss for failure to state a claim.

In order to show that *res ipsa loquitur* applies to a case, a plaintiff must show three things: (i) that an accident was caused by an instrumentality in the exclusive control of a defendant; (ii) that the accident would not occur unless there was unreasonable conduct involved; and (iii) that the plaintiff did not contribute to the accident. As to (i), courts have been lenient to plaintiffs as to the how exclusive the control has to be. As to (ii), a plaintiff need not rule out all other possible explanations for the accident (such as an Act of God), but needs to show it's more likely than not that unreasonable conduct was involved. As to (iii), courts have been more lenient towards plaintiffs—especially with the development of comparative negligence, a topic we discuss in Chapters Eight and Nine. In general, courts have been very hesitant in recent years to apply *res ipsa loquitur*, although no jurisdiction has completely eliminated it as a means of showing breach.

Special Categories of Reasonable People

There are two categories of people subject to special rules for breach: children and people with physical conditions. These two special categories are exceptions to the rule that the reasonable person standard is an objective one that doesn't consider the subjective characteristics of a defendant.

Children. When a child's conduct is being judged under a reasonableness standard, courts apply a reasonable child standard—one that accounts for the age, intelligence, and experience of the particular child. An exception to this rule arises when a child is engaging in adult activity, i.e., conduct that is often undertaken by an adult. If a child is participating in an adult activity, the child is held to a reasonableness standard that doesn't consider the characteristics of the child. What constitutes an adult activity varies from jurisdiction to jurisdiction but can include things like running heavy machinery or equipment and handling firearms. The policy explanation for the "reasonable child" standard is that we want children to learn certain conduct, so we hold them to a lower standard for liability. But adult activity is something we want all individuals to take on with the same degree of care.

Physical condition. If a defendant has a physical condition, like a broken limb, paralysis, or loss of one of the senses, the specific physical condition is considered in setting a standard of care. So, a person with a physical condition is expected to act according to the standard expected of an ordinary person with that condition. Notice, however, that mental conditions are not considered in applying the reasonableness standard. So, a person who is mentally challenged or suffers from a mental disease is held to an objective standard of reasonableness that doesn't consider the mental condition.

■ PROBLEMS ■

---

1. V., a vagrant, wandered into the City of Tarses and found shelter in an abandoned apartment building. He entered the building through a window that had been broken several months before V.'s arrival. V. used the apartment as a place to keep items that he stole during the day. A month after he settled into the abandoned building, V. kidnapped P. and took him back to the apartment, where he killed him for his money and valuables. After the murder, V. left town, never to be seen again.

P's family brings a suit against O., the owner of the abandoned building. The law suit is for negligence and is based on the following ordinance enacted by the City of Tarses three years before the events described:

Sec. 27–11.   Minimum Standards, Responsibilities of Owner

(a) Propery Standards. An owner shall keep the doors and windows of a vacant structure or vacant portion of a structure securely closed to prevent unauthorized entry.

This ordinance was enacted as part of a campaign to encourage property owners to take care of abandoned property and to promote economic renewal and beautification in blighted areas. The ordinance neither expressly creates civil liability nor does it state that civil liability cannot be imposed. Separate penalty provisions of the ordinance state that failure to comply is a criminal misdemeanor, subject to severe fines. Analyze how this statute can be used to establish unreasonableness on the part of O. The jurisdiction in which the case is brought has adopted the rule of negligence per se.

2. Waldo is 16 and lives with his mother in a planned community in the State of Taxing. The biggest amenity in the community is a

large, manmade recreational lake where families in the community come on weekends during the Summer to engage in activities like boating and jet-skiing. Each head of a household in the community must obtain a permit from the community association if they want to use a motorboat or jet ski on the lake. Separate permits are required for motorboats and jet skis. Canoeists and other users of non-motorized vessels do not need a permit. In order to obtain a permit, the head of the household must demonstrate that he or she has taken a course in how to motorboat or jet ski. The permit allows the head and any supervised household member to operate a motorboat or a jet ski on the lake.

Waldo's mother obtained a permit for his family to use a jet ski on the lake. One Saturday afternoon, he and his mother were jet skiing together on the lake. Waldo's mother was close by watching him. At one point, a canoe passed right by Waldo, and Waldo turned sharply to the right to avoid him. The turn was too sharp and Waldo lost control, causing the jet ski to propel ahead unattended before shutting down automatically. Before it shut down, however, the jet ski hit the canoe causing it to capsize. No one was drowned, but the canoe was damaged and the canoeists were soaked and bruised. Other than all this, it was a pretty uneventful Saturday. Analyze the element of breach of duty in the canoeists' negligence claim against Waldo and his mother.

3.   Hank Hill is the supervisor of a painting company. He supervises a crew of one or two workers and often takes on tasks that are very difficult and unusual. For example, one day, he and his employee, Benny, were hired to paint a three story house. One section of the house was above a gravel driveway. Hank placed the ladder in loose gravel in a way that was not very secure. The custom was to place blocks at the base of the ladder when placed on unstable surface like gravel. That day, however, Hank had forgotten to bring the blocks. Nonetheless, Benny climbed to the third floor on the shaky ladder and began painting the area right under the roof. As Benny was climbing down, a rung of the ladder that looked intact suddenly broke for no clear reason, and Benny fell to the ground. Hank ran to the prostrate Benny and noticed that his leg was broken. Benny was otherwise okay. Hank immediately

called for an ambulance. Recalling his first aid training as a boy scout and a member of the National Guard, Hank began applying some alcohol and a tourniquet to places on Benny's leg where he was bleeding. Hank's efforts made Benny pass out from the pain. When Benny woke up, he found himself in a hospital bed with his leg set in a cast. Upon further investigation, Benny learned that Hank's treatments had aggravated his injury, and the doctor had to use a special technique to break his leg further in order for it to heal properly. As a result of Hank's and the doctor's treatments, Benny would probably have only 50% of his leg function after the cast would be removed. Benny sues both Hank and the doctor for negligence. (a) Analyze Benny's arguments for the unreasonableness of Hank and the unreasonableness of the doctor in treating him. (b) Analyze the role of custom in Benny's argument that Hank was unreasonable in how he placed the ladder in the gravel. (c) Analyze Benny's arguments under RIL for Hank's unreasonableness stemming from use of a ladder with a broken rung.

Suggested Answers

1.   If the ordinance is relevant to the facts of the case and O did violate the ordinance, then the violation would establish unreasonableness as a matter of law. If the ordinance is relevant, then the ordinance would also establish a duty on the part of O under tort law. P's family would in addition have to show causation and damages to make the prima facie case for negligence.

As for unreasonableness, P's family would have to show that the ordinance covered the type of injury and class of person at issue in this case. In addition, P's family would have to show that the ordinance established a standard of care and that the violation of the ordinance was not excused or justified. P's family, as plaintiff, would have the burden to show relevance and the violation. O, as defendant, will try to rebut the plaintiff's arguments.

Since the ordinance was enacted to revitalize a blighted part of town, P's family has an argument that the ordinance was designed to prevent the type of crime and violence to person that is at issue in this case. Furthermore, as a crime control statute, the ordinance was meant to protect victims like P from the type of violence perpetrated in this case. In addition, the ordinance lays out a clear standard to be followed: secure all doors and windows of a vacant structure to prevent unauthorized entry. In this case, O had failed to secure the doors and windows as required by statute. Whether O's violation is excused or justified would require knowledge of additional facts. P's family could argue, here, that the statute is written in absolute terms without room for excuse or justification. As a practical matter, however, owners may not be expected to be guarding their property all the time. Nonetheless, the facts suggest that the vagrant had been in the premises for almost a month, during which O did not act to secure his property. In addition, it appears that the window had been broken months before V's entry. These omissions are arguably unjustified and inexcusable.

P's family can anticipate several rebuttals from O. O would first argue that the ordinance is meant to promote economic revitalization and not prevent crime. Criminal statutes exist to deal with the type of events that happened here, and the ordinance was not meant to supplant or complement statutes against murder. Furthermore, the ordinance was meant to protect property owners from loss in property value and not the ordinary citizen from violent felons. Therefore, the statute is not applicable to the case. Even if the statute were applicable, O would argue, the statute does not present a clear standard. The language "securely closed" is arguably vague since due to wear and tear, properties are vulnerable to lapses in security. In addition, the failure to secure a broken window would arguably be excused or justified since the omission is a minor one when the property was otherwise locked.

The hard issues here for the court are those of type of injury and class of persons protected. The court would have to decide whether a ordinance meant to revitalize a blighted area would extend to crime prevention and control. P's family has strong arguments that economic revitalization and crime prevention go hand in hand. O also has a good argument that the ordinance was not meant to replace or complement criminal statutes with civil liability. If the court does find the statute applicable, O's arguments for excuse or justification are weak here given how long the window had been broken without his tending to it.

2.   Canoeist v. Waldo

In order to establish the breach of duty for the negligence claim, the canoeist would have to establish that Waldo committed an unreasonable act. The facts suggest several acts on which to base the claim: the decision to jet ski, the way in which Waldo operated the jet ski, and the sharp turn made to avoid the canoe. Let us focus on the last of the three which seems to be the strongest act on which to base the claim.

The analysis in *Vaughan v. Menlove* suggests that unreasonableness should be based upon practices and knowledge of the relevant community. In assessing whether Waldo turned the jet ski in an unreasonable way, the canoeist would want to start with the custom for moving the jet ski in circumstances like this one. In addition, the canoeist would want to establish notice on Waldo's part, especially his awareness of a canoe being nearby and possibly posing a hazard. The background custom and knowledge would be a part of assessing what a reasonable person would have done under the circumstances. Two factors however complicate the analysis here: (1) Waldo is a child and (2) the emergency situation.

In general, a child is held to the standard of a reasonable person of like age, intelligence, and experience unless the child is engaged in an adult activity. Jet skiing would be considered an adult activity if it is (1) an activity that is dangerous to others, (2) an activity normally undertaken by adults, and (3) an activity for which adult qualifications are required. There may not be much argument about the first element, and the second element is largely an empirical question about the culture and practices in the State of Taxing. The third element is also a question of whether the State of Taxing requires licensure or training and supervision for jet skiing. The facts here refer to the permit requirements of the local community. This may not be relevant to the third element. The facts suggest that the permit requirement may be there to ration the number of boats and jet skis on the lake. However, the permit does limit usage to "supervised household members" and to trained heads of household., suggesting that adult supervision is required for jet skiing. So the first and third factors for adult activity are met, and the second depends upon the culture and practices in State of Taxing. If jet skiing is an adult activity, then Waldo would have to meet the standard of a reasonable adult person. If it is not, Waldo would have to meet the standard of a reasonable 16 year old with his like intelligence and experience.

Finally, the situation involved an emergency in which people would have to make a quick decision that could be deemed unreasonable if they had more time to deliberate. The fact that the situation involved an emergency should also be taken into consideration in assessing what a reasonable adult or reasonable 16 year old with Waldo's intelligence and experience would do.

Canoeist v. Mother

Here the legal theory would be that the Mother acted unreasonably in how she supervised Waldo. Again, unreasonableness would be based on practices and knowledge in the relevant community with regards to supervision of children when they are jet skiing. Here you are told that the mother was close by and watching. If that is all that would be expected of a reasonable person, then the canoeist would not be able to make a prima facie case. In order to make the prima facie case, the canoeist would have to show that a reasonable parent would have done more. To make this case, the plaintiff would need to either find some evidence of practices in supervising children or move on to the types of risk balancing argument in cases like *Carroll Towing*.

3.   (a) The doctor's unreasonableness will be argued in terms of the custom of the medical profession. Benny, as plaintiff, would bring in expert testimony on the proper way to treat his type of injury in an attempt to show that the doctor failed to follow custom. The doctor will bring in expert testimony to show that custom was followed. One complication here is that Benny was unconscious and hence unable to show exactly what the doctor did or failed to do that resulted in his injury (here the loss of function in his leg). *Res ipsa loquitur* would be appropriate here if Benny cannot obtain direct evidence of the doctor's act or omission. *Res ipsa*, in this case,

would satisfy Benny's burden of pleading negligence. A harder question is whether Benny can shift the burden of production to the doctor since Benny was unconscious and the knowledge of what happened in the hospital is with the doctor. In addition, Benny can produce some evidence of improper treatment, such as expert testimony. Therefore, *res ipsa* would be appropriate for pleading, but the burden will remain in with Benny to provide expert testimony that the doctor fell below the custom of the medical profession.

In addition to a medical malpractice claim, Benny would also have an informed consent claim against the doctor potentially. Since Benny was not informed about the medical procedure and did not give his consent to have the procedure performed. However, the doctor has a strong argument here that given an emergency situation and that Benny was passed out, consent could not be obtained. Benny's case will rest in part on whether the doctor could have obtained substituted consent from someone who could have spoken for Benny.

Finally, the negligence case against Hank needs to be contrasted with that against the doctor. The main difference is that custom will not be dispositive for the case against Hank as it would be for the case against the doctor. While Hank has had some first aid training, that would not make him a doctor for the purpose of Benny's claim. Therefore, Benny would have to introduce evidence based on custom, BpL, knowledge, and any relevant statutes to make his case for unreasonableness against Hank.

(b) Benny's argument would be that Hank was unreasonable in placing the ladder on the unstable, gravel surface. Here, the argument would be that industry custom is to use the blocks to stabilize a ladder. Industry custom, however, is not dispositive, except in medical malpractice cases, and therefore would be only one piece of evidence Benny would use to establish unreasonableness. Benny could also use BpL, knowledge, and any relevant statutes to make the case for unreasonableness.

(c) *Res ipsa loquitur* would be appropriate since there is no direct evidence of what made the ladder rung break. If Benny's argument is that Hank was negligent in maintaining the ladder, then *res ipsa loquitur* would help satisfy Benny's burden of pleading. In order to plead *res ipsa loquitur*, Benny would claim that the ladder was in the exclusive control of Hank and that the rung would not have broken absent negligence. Here, exclusive control could be established by the fact that the ladder is part of Hank's business and therefore his responsibility to maintain. The second part may be more difficult since there are many reasons why the rung could have broken (normal wear and tear, etc.). Benny, however, does not have to rule out all of these alternatives at the pleading stage and would have to plead enough to satisfy his burden of pleading. Hank most likely would argue against *res ipsa loquitur* by showing either that the ladder was not in his exclusive control or that there was some other reasons for the rung breaking, other than his negligence. If *res ipsa loquitur* is allowed, then Benny will have met his burden of pleading and the case can move forward.

CHECKLIST FOR BREACH OF DUTY

A.   A plaintiff establishes breach of duty by showing that a defendant's conduct was unreasonable. The standard of reasonableness is meant to be a flexible one that depends on the particular facts of a case and the case's context. The reason the standard is flexible is to allow the law to evolve to reflect changing attitudes, and to allow people to act and conform their conduct to the standard. The major criticism of the reasonableness standard is lack of predictability and notice.

B.   Whether a defendant's conduct is unreasonable is a matter for a jury to decide, although in some instances, when violation of the standard is clear and the courts have had experience with a particular set of facts, the question of reasonableness is a question for a judge, who can take the question away from the jury.

C.   There are five types of arguments that are commonly used to establish the reasonableness of a defendant's conduct. Whenever you are faced with an issue of breach, or the reasonableness of a defendant's conduct, you should work through this list to develop arguments on the side of the plaintiff and the defendant.

1. Custom: The way people usually behave in a particular situation, also known as custom, can be evidence of what is reasonable. Failure to act according to custom can be evidence of acting unreasonably while compliance with custom can be evidence of acting reasonably. Custom, however, is never conclusive evidence of reasonableness except in a medical malpractice case. Evidence of custom provides some basis for determining reasonableness. There is always a question, however, of whether the custom itself is reasonable.

    a. Industry standard is evidence of custom. Non-compliance with industry standards can be evidence of unreasonableness and compliance, evidence of reasonableness. But as with all custom-based evidence, an industry standard is not conclusive.

2. The Hand Formula: The balance of costs and benefits can be evidence of reasonableness. The balancing of costs and benefits is associated with Judge Learned Hand and is often also referred to as the BpL analysis, or BpL test. The B refers to the burden or cost of a particular conduct. The p is the probably of harm that can arise from not following a particular course of conduct and L is the extent of harm that can arise from not following a particular course of conduct. According to the Hand Formula, if B is greater than the p times L (B>pL), then not doing the conduct is reasonable. If B is less than p times L (B<pL), then doing the conduct is reasonable.

3. Statutes: A violation of a statute can be the basis to establish the unreasonableness of a defendant's conduct if (i) the harm a plaintiff suffered is a type of harm the statute was meant to prevent; (ii) the plaintiff is in a class of persons the statute was meant to protect; and (iii) the statute establishes a standard of conduct. If the statute

meets these three criteria, then violation of the statute is negligence per se. In a few jurisdictions, violation of the statute is treated as evidence of unreasonableness, rather than negligence per se.

4. *Res ipsa loquitur*: Sometimes the fact that an accident happened is evidence of unreasonableness—in other words, "the act speaks for itself." *Res ipsa loquitur* applies when (i) an accident occurred as a result of an instrumentality that was in control of a defendant; (ii) the accident is of a type that would not have occurred unless someone had acted unreasonably; and (iii) a plaintiff did not contribute to the accident.

5. Special categories of reasonable people: In general, reasonableness is an objective standard that doesn't consider the special characteristics of a particular defendant. There are two exceptions to this general proposition.

   (a) Children: When a child is being held liable for a non-adult activity, then the age, intelligence, and experience of the child are taken into consideration. If a child, however, is involved in an adult activity, the child's characteristics are not considered and the child's conduct is judged by an objective standard of reasonableness.

   (b) Physical condition: If a defendant has a physical condition, such as loss of sight or loss of a limb, then the physical condition is accounted for in determining the reasonableness of the defendant's conduct. This rule does not apply to any mental conditions of a defendant.

CHAPTER 5

Negligence: Factual and Legal Causation

GENERAL APPROACH

Remember that the plaintiff's case for negligence has four elements: duty, breach, causation, and damages. This chapter turns to the third of these four elements: causation. In order to establish causation, the plaintiff essentially has to show that there is a connection, or nexus, between the defendant's breach and the harm that the plaintiff suffered. Absent such a connection, or nexus, there is no reason to hold the defendant liable for the plaintiff's damages. Suppose that the defendant negligently set a fire and that a strong wind caused the fire to blow onto plaintiff's land damaging his property and person. What caused the harm to the plaintiff? Was is the fire or was it the wind? If the defendant was negligent but the harm was not the result of the defendant's unreasonable conduct, then holding the defendant liable is inconsistent with the compensation and deterrence goals of tort law.

There are two things that plaintiff must show in order to establish causation: factual causation and legal causation. Factual causation has to do with what actually (as a matter of fact) caused the plaintiff's injuries. Legal causation has to do with the desirable policy of holding defendant liable for plaintiff's harm. Legal causation deals with cases where the injury to the plaintiff is so great or so remotely connected to the defendant's unreasonable conduct that imposing liability is inconsistent with the goals of tort law. Suppose that defendant was negligent in setting a fire and that fire is the factual cause of injury to the plaintiff. But also suppose the fire spread to burn down the entire block or town. Should the defendant be liable for all the damages that were factually caused by the fire? At one level, it might seem to be the correct policy to hold the defendant liable for all the harm that was caused in this example. But as a practical matter, holding the defendant liable for everything might not be enforceable. Furthermore, there might have been harm that resulted but could have been avoided if the injured party had been more careful. The requirement of legal causation recognizes that there needs to be some limit on the scope of a defendant's liability. Therefore, under the doctrine of legal causation, the defendant is liable only for the harm that is not the remote consequence of the defendant's unreasonable conduct.

This chapter discusses factual and legal causation as the two parts of the causation requirement for a negligence claim. You should remember that the element of causation has two parts and that they fit together to establish the connection, or nexus, between the defendant's breach and the injury suffered by the plaintiff.

FACTUAL CAUSATION

A plaintiff must show that defendant's unreasonable conduct was the factual cause of the plaintiff's injuries. This means that plaintiff's injury can be traced back to defendant's unreasonable conduct. If the defendant can show that something other than the unreasonable conduct caused the injuries, then the plaintiff has not established causation.

A very simple example of factual causation is provided by a defendant hitting the plaintiff's car through unreasonable driving. When defendant's car hit plaintiff's car, the car itself was probably damaged by the collision. But if defendant can show that some or all of the damage to the car existed before the collision, then the defendant's unreasonable conduct is not the factual cause of plaintiff's injuries and therefore the plaintiff has failed to show causation. Personal injuries can be more complicated because defendant's unreasonable conduct may have aggravated an existing physical condition of the plaintiff. Suppose that in the car collision example, the plaintiff has sprained his leg before the accident, but the collision caused the leg to break. Then, defendant would have cause the plaintiff's injuries because the unreasonable conduct made the plaintiff's condition worse.

Law school exams and real world cases often contain complicated causation issues. The best way to deal with these sometimes bizarre and strange fact patterns is to break them down into the parts of causation. First, consider factual causation issues, then consider legal causation issues. As for the factual causation issues, separate out the case of a single cause from that of multiple causes. Also, keep in mind that the issue of factual causation often invites questions of uncertainty. We will address these three sub-issues in turn.

Single Cause: But for test

If there is only one possible cause of plaintiff's injury, then courts apply the but for test to see if the plaintiff is able to establish that defendant's unreasonable conduct is the factual cause of the injuries. Under the but for test, a plaintiff must show that if the defendant had not engaged in the unreasonable conduct, then the injuries would not have occurred. Put another way, "but for" the defendant's conduct, plaintiff would not have been injured. The test requires the plaintiff to work with a hypothetical scenario, one based on the defendant not having acted unreasonably. This scenario, however, can also be presented in the positive. Suppose the defendant had acted reasonably. Then the circumstances would have been different and the accident, and therefore the injury, would not have occurred. The defendant will be trying to show that the cause of the plaintiff's injury was some other factor, perhaps the plaintiff's conduct or perhaps a third party who was also involved in the accident.

Consider the example of the automobile accident. The plaintiff will try to show that if the defendant had not acted unreasonably (or put in the positive, the defendant acted reasonably), then the accident would not have occurred and therefore the plaintiff would not have been injured. The defendant, however, will try to show that some other factor caused the accident. Perhaps the car was defective or the road conditions were poor. Alternatively, perhaps the plaintiff was driving poorly and did not take proper precautions while driving. Whichever side can make the strongest case based on the evidence will win on this issue. Remember, however, that the plaintiff has the burden of proof and has to establish it with a preponderance of the evidence, meaning that the plaintiff's case has to be slightly stronger than the defendant's.

Often scientific testimony will be important in factual causation cases. The use of scientific testimony will be crucial, for example, in a toxic torts case (involving hazardous substances) or in a products liability case (involving faulty tires or faulty brakes). In such cases, the issue of factual causation will become a battle of the experts and will require the judge or the jury to weight the competing scientific testimony. Your Torts class may talk in more detail about the use of scientific testimony in Torts cases. If you do not cover the issue of scientific testimony in your Torts class, you will cover it in an evidence class. You should, however, be aware of how the issue arises in the context of factual causation. We will discuss the issue of scientific evidence under the sub-issue of uncertainty below.

Multiple Cause: Substantial factor test

In many cases, a plaintiff's injury was very clearly the result of multiple causes. One example of this situation arises when there is a natural cause and the unreasonable conduct of defendant that both arguably contributed to the plaintiff's injury. For example,. a defendant's unreasonable conduct may have started a fire that went onto the plaintiff's property. At the same time, however, a fire caused by lightning also damages the plaintiff's property. Is the defendant not liable in this case because the natural fire would have damaged the plaintiff's property anyway? If so, the defendant has had a lucky break. Another example is when there are multiple defendants all of whom have done something unreasonable. In such situation, can each defendant claim that the particular unreasonable conduct was not the cause of the plaintiff's injury? If so, then all the defendants can escape liability because no one defendant was the but for cause of the injuries.

These examples illustrate the problem with the "but for" test when there are multiple causes. Because of this deficiency, courts use the "substantial factor" test when multiple causes are involved. Under the substantial factor test, a defendant's unreasonable conduct is the factual cause of plaintiff's injury if the plaintiff can show that the conduct was a substantial factor in causing the accident. Substantial factor is admittedly a vague term. The test is meant to give the plaintiff, and the court, some flexibility in determining when a defendant's unreasonable conduct gives rise to liability when there are multiple factors that lead to the plaintiff's injury. In cases involving scientific testimony, statistical evidence is often used to establish using probabilities what the relative contributions of the various factors are to the plaintiff's injury. If, for example, the plaintiff was exposed to a toxic substance, medical and other scientific evidence will often provide some statistical basis for measuring the substantial factor. These cases often do boil down to a battle of the experts. In cases not involving scientific testimony, a judge or jury will look to the evidence to see how likely it is that defendant's unreasonable conduct contributed to the plaintiff's injuries in light of all the circumstances. The issue of factual causation will be very fact specific.

There is a special case of multiple causes and the substantial factor test associated with the famous case of *Summers v. Tice*, 199 P.2d 1 (1948). Remember in that case that two defendants shot a rifle in the direction of the plaintiff. Buckshot from one of the rifles injured the plaintiff. There was no question that both defendants were unreasonable in shooting the plaintiff. The difficult issue was determining which one of the two defendants was the factual cause of the injury. In such a case where each defendant was equally likely to be the factual cause, the court created a new rule that shifted the burden to each of the defendants to show that his unreasonable conduct was not the factual cause of the injury. If neither defendant can disprove being the factual cause, then liability is split evenly among the defendants.

A variation of the *Summers v. Tice* rule arises under the rule of market share liability that is sometimes applied in products liability cases. If a plaintiff cannot show which of the many manufacturers produced the product that injured the plaintiff, then the burden shifts to each manufacturer to show that it was not the producer of the product that injured the plaintiff. The manufacturer can meet this burden by pointing to characteristics of its product or the timing of sales that precluded its product from being the one that injured the plaintiff. Among the manufacturers who cannot meet the burden to disprove it was the producer, liability is split according to the market share of the respective manufacturers at the time of injury.

As the discussion of *Summers v. Tice* and market share liability show, the issue of factual causation with multiple factors is closely connected to the issue of how liability is apportioned among the defendants. We will discuss the issue of apportionment in more detail in Chapter Nine, when we discuss the defense of comparative negligence. Comparative negligence adopts some of the apportionment rules from *Summers. v. Tice* and the market share liability cases.

Factual Causation and the Problem of Uncertainty

Your Torts class might study the issues of uncertainty and statistical evidence as they arise in the area of factual causation. These issues are difficult and can be daunting. Many courts have shied away from the issue of uncertainty and tort law, rejecting doctrines such as loss of chance. This book will not go into this topic because of a current trend in the law to move away from these issues by requiring more from the plaintiff before allowing a case to proceed or allowing the plaintiff to succeed on the merits. If your class goes into these topics in more detail, the word of advice is to to focus on how these topics arise in the context of factual causation. Except in rare circumstances, we cannot know with certainty what caused plaintiff's injury. In complex torts cases, there may be multiple factors at work. Tort law deals with this uncertainty by placing the burden on the plaintiff to bring in enough supporting evidence that weighs slightly more heavily than the supporting evidence of the defendant. In other words, factual causation can be a very fact intensive inquiry that takes into consideration the circumstances in which the defendant's unreasonable conduct occurred.

LEGAL CAUSATION

The second part of the causation requirement is legal causation, also known as proximate causation. The plaintiff must show as the third element of the claim for negligence that the defendant's unreasonable conduct was both the factual and legal causation of the injuries. This book will use the term legal causation to contrast it with factual causation. You should understand that legal causation and proximate causation refer to the same concept. You should also keep in mind that for the plaintiff to establish causation, both factual causation and legal causation must be shown.

Keep in mind that the requirement of legal causation is a question of policy. Sometimes a defendant's unreasonable conduct might lead to quite extensive injuries. Injuring a plaintiff might result not only in hospital bills but also in the loss of a promising career as a professional football player. Should the defendant be liable for all the millions of dollars the plaintiff suffers as a result of the defendant's unreasonable conduct? Alternatively, a defendant's unreasonable conduct might result in a entire highway shutting down or an entire town burning to the ground? Should the defendant be liable for all those injuries as well? The requirement of legal causation places some boundaries on the scope of the defendant's liability to the plaintiff. Keep in mind that other legal rules also serve this function of placing boundaries on the defendant's liability. The duty rules discussed in Chapter Three exclude, in some cases, emotional injury and pure economic loss from the scope of defendant's liability. In the next chapter on recoverable damages, we will discuss rules about what types of damages the plaintiff can recover. The requirement of legal causation is another example of how a defendant's liability is limited by the law for purposes of fairness and effective administration of tort law.

There are two tests that courts typically use for determining whether a defendant's unreasonable conduct is the legal cause of the plaintiff's injuries: the directness test and foreseeability test. Each test developed separately in the law, and each is independent of the other. When analyzing a legal causation issue, you should apply each test to the facts you are given. Keep in mind, however, that in most cases, each test will lead to the same result for reasons we discuss below.

Directness test

Under the directness test, a defendant's unreasonable conduct is the legal cause of the plaintiff's injuries if the injuries are the direct consequence of the conduct. The plaintiff needs to show that there is a direct connection between the injuries and conduct. If there is an intervening cause in the chain of events between the conduct and the injuries, then that intervening cause can cut off liability to the defendant if the intermediate cause is unforeseeable. An unforeseeable intervening cause is called superseding because it supersedes the liability of the defendant.

The classic example of the directness case is provided by *In re Polemis*, 3 K.B. 560 (1921), a decision you will very likely read or discuss in your Torts class. In *Polemis*, workers on a ship dropped a wooden plan while working at the top of the ship. The plank fell into the hold of the ship where the plank struck the sides of the ship causing a flame to ignite. The flame made some gas that was in the hold of the ship catch fire causing the ship to burn down. The ship at the time was being rented, and the owners sued the renters for damages to the ship under a negligence theory. The court found that the dropping of the plank was unreasonable conduct and that this conduct was the legal cause of the fire. Notice that there was no issue of factual causation in this case. If the plank had not fallen, then under the circumstances the ship would not have caught fire. The issue was whether the dropping of the plank was the legal cause. The court concluded it was under the directness test.

There are two points to understand about the directness test. The first is how the test is applied. In *Polemis*, the plaintiff could establish a chain of events that connected the unreasonable conduct with the injury. Essentially the chain looked like this: plank falls then goes into hold setting off a spark then spark ignites the gas and then the explosion from the gas made the ship catch fire. The court found no superseding cause in this case, and therefore the defendant's unreasonable conduct was the legal cause of the injuries. In general, under the directness test, the plaintiff establishes a direct chain from the unreasonable conduct to the injury without any superseding causes. The defendant, on the other hand, tries to break the chain in the plaintiff's presentation of the evidence to establish a superseding cause that cuts off liability.

What are examples of intervening causes under the directness test? Suppose a defendant acting unreasonably hits a plaintiff's automobile causing a non-fatal injury to the plaintiff's person. An ambulance picks up the plaintiff to take him to the hospital. On the trip to the hospital, the ambulance enters into an accident resulting in the death of the plaintiff. For the sake of this example, assume that the ambulance accident was not the result of anyone's unreasonable conduct. Is the defendant liable for the death of the plaintiff when the initial collision caused only a non-fatal injury? The ambulance accident is an example of an intervening cause. Whether this intervening cause is also superseding and therefore cuts off the liability of the defendant depends on whether the court finds the automobile accident to have been foreseeable. More on what foreseeability means below. For understanding the directness test at this point, use this example to understand what we mean by an intervening cause and understand that an intervening cause that is unforeseeable is a superseding cause.

The second point to remember about the directness test is the policy justification. The directness test reinforces the compensation and deterrence goals of tort law. If plaintiff's injuries can be traced to the defendant's unreasonable conduct, then the plaintiff should be compensated by the defendant. If there is no direct connection, then the plaintiff has to obtain compensation for the injuries from some source other than the defendant. Furthermore, if a defendant knows that there will be liability for all direct consequences of the unreasonable conduct, then this potentially broad liability will serve as a strong deterrent for the defendant to act reasonably. The only hope that an unreasonable defendant has is there is a superseding cause that will be found to cut off liability. But since by definition, a superseding cause is unforeseeable, cutting off liability with a superseding cause does not interfere with the deterrence goals of tort law.

One obvious point from the discussion of the directness test is how foreseeability creeps into the analysis on the issue of superseding cause. Under the directness test, foreseeability arises when an intervening cause cuts off liability. Some courts express this point by stating that the directness test requires a plaintiff to show that defendant's unreasonable conduct is the direct cause of the plaintiff's injury and there is no unforeseeable intervening cause. Foreseeability becomes relevant when there is an intervening cause that defendant claims should cut off liability. If such an intervening cause exists, then the plaintiff must show that the intervening cause was foreseeable. If the intervening cause was unforeseeable, then the intervening cause supersedes the defendant's liability. Because of the role of foreseeability in the directness test, it is often the case that the directness test and foreseeability test often lead to the same result in the legal causation analysis. But more about this relationship after we discuss the foreseeability test in the following section.

Foreseeability test

Under the foreseeabilty test, a plaintiff must show that the injuries are the foreseeable consequence of the defendant's unreasonable conduct. In applying the foreseeability test, courts sometimes state that the plaintiff's injuries cannot be too remote from the defendant's unreasonable conduct. The use of the word remote suggests the directness test discusses above. But in using the word remote, courts are suggesting the plaintiff's injuries are too remote in time, amount, or type in relationship to the defendant's unreasonable conduct for the defendant to have foreseen the injuries. Therefore, the defendant is not the legal cause of the injuries.

First, try to understand how the foreseeability test works. The classic cases are the *Wagon Mound (No. 1)*, UKPC 1 (1961), and *Wagon Mound (No. 2)*, 1 A.C. 617 (1967), decisions that you most likely will read or discuss in your Torts class. Both cases are based on the same facts, but each involved different plaintiffs. The facts are as follows. The Wagon Mound was a ship that spilled oil in the harbor of a port in Australia. The ship did not clean the oil spill, and shortly after the spill, workers on the dock were welding. Sparks from the welding ignited the oil, and the resulting fire caused the dock and several ships in the harbor to burn. In *Wagon Mound 1*, the plaintiff was the owner of the dock whose workers were welding. In *Wagon Mound 2*, the plaintiffs were the ship owners whose ships burned in the fire. These cases are interesting because the results were different in the two cases. In *Wagon Mound 1*, the plaintiffs lost while in *Wagon Mound 2*, they won. One explanation for the different results has to do with the legal causation analysis under the foreseeability test.

In *Wagon Mound 1*, the court analyzed the legal causation issue under the foreseeability test. The court reasoned that the fire to the harbor was too remote from the oil spill. Specifically, the court found that the owner of the Wagon Mound could not have foreseen that someone would have worked with fire so close to the oil spill. Therefore, the injury to the harbor owner's own property from the fire was not a foreseeable consequence of the oil spill. In *Wagon Mound 2*, the court, however, found that a fire in the harbor could have been foreseen, although the particular way in which the fire occurred might not have been. Therefore, the fire to the ships in the harbor was the foreseeable consequence of the Wagon Mound's unreasonable conduct of spilling oil in the harbor.[1] One explanation for the two cases is the court's view of what consequences are foreseeable for a particular unreasonable conduct.

One interesting point of the *Wagon Mound 1* decision is the court's explicit criticism of the *Polemis* decision, which is described as archaic. The court's criticism is aimed at a very literal application of the directness test by the courts. Under the facts of the *Wagon Mound* cases, the plaintiffs argued that Wagon Mound was the legal

---

1. One explanation for *Wagon Mound 2* is that the court was focusing on the issue of whether spilling oil in the harbor was an unreasonable act. That reading is correct to the extent that the court does extensively discuss the reasonableness of the Wagon Mound's conduct. However, this explanation is not completely satisfactory. The court does find Wagon Mound liable for negligence in the second case which means the court must have found all four elements of negligence, including causation.

cause of the fire because the fire could be directly traced to the oil spill. The *Wagon Mound 1* court, however, rejects this literal application of the directness test. As the court states, liability is potentially unlimited under the directness test. The foreseeability test, according to the court, does a better, and more fair, job of limiting the defendant's liability to the foreseeable consequences of the unreasonable conduct. And, as we noted in the previous paragraph, the court concluded that the harm to the harbor was too remote (or unforeseeable) and the harm to the ships was not.

The *Wagon Mound 1* court, however, was perhaps interpreting the directness test too literally. After all, superseding causes do cut off liability to the defendant. Although the court did not analyze the cases in this way, both *Wagon Mound* cases can be analyzed under the directness test. In *Wagon Mound 1*, the sparks from the welding would be the superseding the cause the cuts off liability to the defendant for the harm to the harbor. In *Wagon Mound 2*, however, the sparks were intervening but not foreseeable. The court in *Wagon Mound 2* is saying that the owner of the Wagon Mound could have foreseen a fire starting somehow and burning the ships. In *Wagon Mound 1*, the court is implicitly saying that Wagon Mound could not have foreseen that the harbor owner's workers would have welded near an oil spill and burned its own harbor.

These cases have confused students ever since they started to appear in Torts casebooks. The issue of legal causation confuses practitioners because it seems so unpredictable and comes across as after the fact reasoning. A court can reach any result they want to under the legal causation requirement. In practice, this last fear has a kernel of truth in it, as your discussion of the topic in class will undoubtedly show. While all this discussion of legal causation might be frustrating, keep in mind the good news as a law student: you are not working on a real case for a real client to whom you have to explain how unpredictable legal causation might be. Instead, as a law student, you need to show that you understand the various tests and be able to apply each test to the facts you are given. In analyzing a legal causation issue, point out the role of legal causation in giving some boundaries to the scope of the defendant's liability and the two tests, directness and foreseeability, that courts have devised to determine the extent of a defendant's liability for unreasonable conduct.

Legal Policy: Perspectives on Palsgraf

Let us recap what we have covered under the topic of legal causation. Legal causation, also known as proximate causation, is the second part of the causation element of a negligence claim. The purpose of legal causation is to place some bounds on the extent of a defendant's liability. Courts have devised two tests to analyze legal causation: the directness test and the foreseeability test. Under the directness test, a plaintiff has to establish a chain from the defendant's unreasonable conduct to the plaintiff's injuries. If there are any intervening causes in this chain, plaintiff must show that the intervening cause was foreseeable to the defendant. Under the foreseeability test, a plaintiff has to establish that the injuries were the foreseeable consequence of the unreasonable conduct. Put another way, under the foreseeability test, the plaintiff's injury cannot be too remote, in time, amount or type from the defendant's unreasonable conduct.

As we discussed in the previous section, the directness and foreseeability test can often lead to the same result depending on one applies the tests. Ultimately, the legal causation part of causation is a matter of legal policy. A court finds legal causation when a defendant should be liable and does not find it when a defendant should not be liable. But, what is the legal policy that informs courts in determining legal causation? This big question is what comes up in the famous case of *Palsgraf v. Long Island Railroad*, 162 N.E. 99 (N.Y. 1928), perhaps the classic case of the law of Torts.

In *Palsgraf*, plaintiff sued the Long Island Railroad for injuries sustained while being injured by falling scales on the railroad platform. The series of events were as follows. There was a rush on the platform as passengers were boarding the train during the Fourth of July holidays. A railway attendant pushed a passenger holding a parcel onto the train. The parcel fell out of the passenger's hands, and because they contained fireworks, they set off an explosion when they hit the tracks. The explosion caused a combination of sound vibrations and panicked crowds which made the scales come lose and fall on Mrs. Palsgraf.

After reading this synopsis of the facts, you may seem skeptical about the plaintiff's claim for negligence against the railroad. Certainly Judge Cardozo was. In the rhetorical flourish of his opinion, he finds for the railroad, holding that the injury was not foreseeable. Judge Cardozo's analysis is a confusing one with its analysis of both legal causation and duty issues. The Judge concludes that the lack of foreseeability means that there is no duty. But his opinion also analyzes the lack of legal causation. Consequently, one reading of the decision is that it is really about duty. A more accurate reading would be that Judge Cardozo is saying that the issue of legal causation can be matter for the judge when the consequences are so unforeseeable. It is on this point that Judge Andrews differs from Judge Cardozo. Judge Andrews sees issues in the legal causation that may be appropriate for the jury to decide. For Judge Andrews, a judge needs to be careful about the implicit policy judgments that are being made when a judge concludes that legal causation does not exist.

What are the policy concerns? The one we have talked about in general under legal causation is ensuring that liability is not unbounded, a potential problem if causation required only a showing of factual causation. But more specifically, as the *Palsgraf* decision particularly shows, the legal causation analysis rests on the issue of what risks are the foreseeable consequences of the defendant's unreasonable conduct. To conclude that an unreasonable act is the legal cause of an injury is to say that the injury is the type of risk that we want the defendant to protect against. The law of negligence by imposing liability on a defendant for legally causing an injury to the plaintiff is concluding that the defendant can and should alter conduct in order to prevent the risk of that injury occurring. In *Wagon Mound 1*, for example, the court found no liability because the harbormaster could have protected itself by managing the welding more carefully. In *Wagon Mound 2*, on the other hand, the court finds liability because the owner of Wagon Mound should have cleaned up the oil spill in order to prevent the fire that burned the ship. In *Palsgraf*, Judge Cardozo concludes that there was nothing the railroad could have done to protect Palsgraf from the exploding firecrackers. Judge Andrews, on the other hand, was not so sure.

In analyzing legal causation, you should be attuned to these policy concerns. You should also be attuned to how attorneys and judges grapple with these issues in handling real cases. One example of how these issues arise is the egg shell plaintiff rule. Under this rule, a defendant is liable for the physical injuries suffered by the plaintiff no matter how unforeseeable. For example, in *Steinhauser v. Hertz Corp.*, 421 F.2d 1169 (2d Cir. 1970), plaintiff suffered psychological trauma after being in an automobile accident caused by defendant's unreasonable conduct. The court reasoned that, as long as factual causation was shown for the psychological trauma, defendant would be liable because a defendant takes the plaintiff as given. For policy reasons, the court ruled that just as a defendant might luck out if the plaintiff is physically strong and not injured badly by an automobile accident so a defendant bears the risk of the plaintiff being particularly sensitive physically. The egg shell plaintiff rule is an application of the directness test for legal causation, and courts adopt this approach for the policy reasons of protecting more physically vulnerable plaintiffs.

On a final note, it is worth pointing out that the egg shell plaintiff does not apply to property losses. If a defendant's unreasonably drives his car into plaintiff's car and breaks the expensive Ming vase and equipment in the trunk of plaintiff's car, then the defendant can argue against liability for the damage to the vase and equipment for lack of foreseeability. In other words, foreseeability can limit the scope of defendant's liability for property damage but not for physical injury The reason for this difference is a policy of protecting physically vulnerable plaintiffs and recognizing that with property damage, the plaintiff may be in a better position to protect against damage to particularly valuable property that can be lost due to the unreasonable conduct of others.

■ PROBLEMS ■

1. Hank Hill is the supervisor of a painting company. He supervises a crew of one or two workers and often takes on tasks that are very difficult and unusual. For example, one day, he and his employee, Benny, were hired to paint a three story house. One section of the house was above a gravel driveway. Hank placed the ladder in loose gravel in a way that was not very secure. The custom was to place blocks at the base of the ladder when placed on unstable surface like gravel. That day, however, Hank had forgotten to bring the blocks. Nonetheless, Benny climbed to the third floor on the shaky ladder and began painting the area right under the roof. As Benny was climbing down, a rung of the ladder that looked intact suddenly broke for no clear reason, and Benny fell to the ground. Hank ran to the prostrate Benny and noticed that his leg was broken. Benny was otherwise okay. Hank immediately called for an ambulance. Recalling his first aid training as a boy scout and a member of the National Guard, Hank began applying some alcohol and a tourniquet to places on Benny's leg where he was bleeding. Hank's efforts made Benny pass out from the pain. When Benny woke up, he found himself in a hospital bed with his leg set in a cast. Upon further investigation, Benny learned that Hank's treatments had aggravated his injury, and the doctor had to use a special technique to break his leg further in order for it to heal properly. As a result of Hank's and the doctor's treatments, Benny would probably have only 50% of his leg function after the cast would be removed. Benny sued both Hank and the doctor for negligence. Identify all the acts that lead to Benny's injury. (A) Which of these arguably caused the injury and which did not? (B) Analyze Benny's arguments for causation in his negligence claim against (1) Hank and (2) the doctor.

2. Shop Co is a grocery store at the corner of Elm Street and Main Street. There is a driveway entrance off of Main Street into the parking lot for the store. There is no access to the parking lot from Elm Street. Shop Co has several employees, one of whose duties is to collect shopping carts that have been left in the parking lot after

customers have loaded their car and left. Many stores have stalls where customers can place their empty shopping carts. To save on costs, Shop Co. has not built such stalls. One Monday, the employee whose duty is to collect shopping carts calls in sick. As a result, shopping carts become piled up in the parking lot. That Monday is a particularly windy day, and the wind carries one of the carts into the middle of Main Street. Paul Plaintiff is driving down Main Street when the shopping cart stops in front of him in his lane. In order to avoid hitting the cart, Paul tries to drive around it, but is unable to do so successfully and unavoidably hits the cart causing damage to his car. The car behind Paul, that was driving safely, runs into Paul's car causing Paul to hit his head against the steering wheel. Analyze Paul's argument against Shop Co that the grocery store's unreasonable acts caused his injuries.

Suggested Answers

1. (A) The relevant acts would be (i) the ladder was placed on gravel, (ii) the rung broke, (iii) Hank treated Benny, (iv) the doctor treated Benny. Each of these could have been a factual cause of the injury. The ladder being placed on gravel could have lead to the rung breaking. The rung breaking clearly lead to Benny falling. The treatments then caused the broken leg to be made worse. Benny might have a difficult time establishing factual causation for the ladder being placed on gravel because the connection between the rickety ladder that may have loosened the rung is somewhat weak. Finally, each of these acts arguably could have directly and foreseeably resulted in Benny's injury. Once again, placing the ladder on gravel might be a weak basis for proximate cause. Furthermore, the negligent treatment by the doctor might be an intervening and superseding cause that cuts off Hank's liability from the broken rung and the negligent treatment.

(B) (1) Benny v. Hank: There are three unreasonable acts that Benny could use to build his case for negligence against Hank: (a) placing the ladder in unstable gravel; (b) the broken ladder; (c) the treatment of the leg

(a) Placing the ladder in unstable gravel: Benny's argument for causation would have to be that the unstableness of the ladder was the factual and proximate cause of Benny's injury. Benny will have some difficulty with factual cause. Under the but for test, Benny would have to show that if the ladder had not been placed in the gravel, he would not have fallen and broken his leg. This connection may be difficult to show since the ladder rung may have broken away, resulting in his fall. If Benny uses the placement of the ladder in gravel as the unreasonable, he would have to show that the instability either factually caused the rung to break or for him to fall. Assuming he can do that and establish factual causation from the placement in the gravel to the fall, Benny would still have problems with proximate causation. For the placement in the gravel to be the proximate cause of the injury, Benny would have to show that the placement directly and foreseeably resulted in the injury. Here, assuming that the instability of the ladder resulted in the fall, the injury to the leg would be the usual consequence of such a fall. Hank might argue that the treatment by the doctor is a superseding and intervening cause that would cut off his liability. Benny has a good argument that the alleged improper treatment by the doctor would be the foreseeable consequence of the injury: Hank could have foreseen that Benny would go to hospital. In fact Hank called the ambulance. Furthermore, Hank could have foreseen that an injury in the hospital could occur. As discussed below with respect to the doctor, Hank's liability would not cut off the doctor's liability for any malpractice claim.

(b) Ladder breaking: Benny has a strong argument that the broken rung was the factual cause of his injury. If the rung had not broken, Benny very likely would not have fallen. As far proximate cause, a broken leg would be the direct and foreseeable consequence of such a fall. The arguments above regarding the doctor's treatment as a superseding and intervening cause would also apply here.

(c) Hank's treatment: If Hank's treatment was unreasonable, then Benny has a good argument for factual causation. The difficulty here is that both Hank and the doctor treated Benny and there is an issue of whose treatment factually caused Benny's injury.

They both contributed, but the doctor would most likely testify that Hank's treatment aggravated Benny's injury. Benny can address these questions through expert testimony about the respective treatments and attempt to disentangle the complicated factual causation issues. Alternatively, a creative court might apply the rule of *Summers v. Tice* and shift the burden of persuasion to Hank and the doctor for each to show that he was not the factual cause of the accident. The facts are not dissimilar from *Summers*, except here Benny can in theory rely on expert evidence to show which tortfeasor caused what. However, courts have recently looked at *Summers* with some disfavor, leaving the burden on the plaintiff to meet the burden of persuasion and dismissing against the plaintiff if he is unsuccessful. Finally, as far as proximate cause, if Hank's treatment is the factual causation, the arguments above about superseding and intervening cause would apply here as well.

(2) Benny v. Doctor: Benny would have rely on expert testimony to identify the doctor's treatment fell below the custom of the profession. If Benny can show how the doctor fell below the standard of care, Benny would then have to show that the doctor's treatment was the factual and proximate cause of the injury. The analysis of factual causation above under Hank's treatment would apply here. If Benny can show that the doctor's treatment was the factual cause of the injury, Benny would have to show that the extent of injury was the direct and foreseeable consequence of the treatment. On this point, Benny could point to what the profession knows about the possible risks from the type of treatment the doctor adopted. The doctor will most likely argue that Benny's loss of use of his legs was factually caused by Hank's treatment or that the extent of it was unusual and unforeseeable from his treatment.

2.   OUTLINE OF ANSWER: We present this answer as an outline to give you a sense of how to put together an answer before you actually write it out on for an exam.

I.   Failure to have a stall

  A.   Unreasonable?

    1.   Custom: not dispositive. Paul has an argument that

many stores have installed them. Shop Co would argue that not all stores have and that the custom itself is unreasonable since it encourages people to leave carts out in the parking lot.

2. Knowledge: Paul would look to previous incidents that would place Shop Co on notice. Also Paul can appeal to common knowledge that shopping carts roll off. Shop Co can point to lack of previous episodes or unusual circumstances.

3. BPL analysis: Paul would point to low cost of install-ing stalls as compared to probability of injury and its extent. Shop Co would point out high cost, low probability and low extent of injury.

4. Statute: no statute on point requiring stalls or regu-lating shopping carts.

5. RIL: here not relevant since Paul can identify act or omission that caused the accident.

B. Causation?

1. Factual causation: Paul would have to show that if there had been a stall the shopping cart would not have been blown away by the wind. Paul's argument would rest on showing that people are more likely to put away the cart in the stall or that the wind could not lift the cart from the stall. Shop Co's argument is that either there will always be someone who would not put the cart away or that the wind could have separated the cart from the stall anyway. Note that under this approach, the wind would not be a separate and independent cause because the failure to place the stall is not simultaneous with the wind blowing the cart into the road.

2. Proximate causation: If the failure to install a stall is a factual causation, the next question is whether Paul's injury is a direct and foreseeable consequence of the failure to have a stall. Here, Paul will argue that a loose cart in the parking lot could very likely roll into the street given the location of the store and the lose cart could have caused a car accident, as occurred here. Shop Co. would argue that Paul's negligence

in avoiding the cart and the rear end collision with the car driving behind were the cause of the accident. If Paul were negligent, then Shop Co would have the complete defense of contributory negligence in jurisdictions that recognize that defense. Absent Paul's negligence, Paul has the argument that his avoidance and the rear end were not superseding and intervening causes since both would be foreseeable from the cart rolling into the street. Neither are unusual results or unusual means for a car accident.

II. Failure to remove lose carts from parking lot

    A. Unreasonable?

        1. Custom: Paul would look to see what other stores do to collect lose carts and replace sick employees. Shop Co would argue that it had a system in place to remove lose carts, but on that day its employee was unfortunately sick.

        2. Knowledge: Paul can point to the fact that Shop Co knew the employee in charge of the carts was sick that day and therefore carts were not being picked up from the lot. Furthermore, Paul can point to the fact that it was a windy day and that the wind can move carts. Shop Co. can point to any incidents of loose carts going into the traffic as it did here.

        3. BpL: Paul would point to the low cost of having someone pick up the carts or at least requesting customers to pick up carts after themselves relative to the probability and the extent of injury. Shop Co would point to the low probability of carts rolling into the street and the high costs of finding a replacement for the employee or collecting the carts.

        4. Statute: none on point.

        5. RIL: not relevant here.

    B. Causation?

        1. Factual causation: The arguments here are similar to the arguments over the stall.

2.   Proximate causation: similar to discussion above.

III. Cart rolling into street itself

A. Unreasonable?

1.   RIL: would apply here if Paul cannot show what it is that Shop Co did or failed to do. To meet his burden of pleading through RIL, Paul would show that the carts were in the exclusive control of Shop Co and that the accident would not occur absent negligence. As for the first part, since the carts were on Shop Co's property and part of its business, exclusive control can be established by pointing out that Shop Co had responsibility for the carts. As for the second part of RIL, Paul can point to the unusualness of the carts rolling into streets and the unreasonable hazard the cart rolling into the street poses for drivers to support an argument that negligence must have been involved. Notice that RIL in this case would allow Paul to satisfy his burden of pleading, allowing him to get past a motion to dismiss and into discovery in order to develop his evidence against Shop Co to establish the unreasonable act or omission by the store.

B. Causation?

1.   Factual causation: See above. Note that Paul would have to pinpoint what it is that Shop Co did or failed to do in order to develop the causation argument.

2.   Proximate causation: similar to discussion above.

CHECKLIST FOR CAUSATION

A. Causation: plaintiff must show that the defendant's unreasonable conduct caused the injury suffered by the plaintiff. Causation requires showing a connection, or nexus, between the defendant's unreasonable act and the injury. There are two parts to causation: factual causation and legal causation.

B. Factual causation: requires the plaintiff to show that there is a factual connection between the unreasonable conduct and the injury. Courts have devised tests for factual causation based upon the number of causes at issue in a case.

    1. Single cause: if there is only one cause for the injury, then courts apply the but for test for factual causation. Under the but for test, plaintiff must show that but for the defendant's unreasonable conduct, the injury would not have occurred.

    2. Multiple causes: if there are possibly more than one cause for the injury, then courts apply the substantial factor test for factual causation. Under the substantial factor test, plaintiff must show that the defendant's unreasonable act was more likely thank other factors to have caused the plaintiff's injury.

        a. Special case of *Summers v. Tice*: when there are multiple defendants and each are equally likely to have caused the accident, then the burden shifts to each defendant to show that they were not the substantial factor. Absent this special rule, all the defendants could be found to be not liable even though one of them must have caused the injury. A special application of the *Summers v. Tice* rule is market share liability: when a product caused a harm but the plaintiff cannot show which manufacturer produced the specific product that the plaintiff used, then each manufacturer will be held liable for the damages based on market share. Under the market share liability rule, each manufacturer will have the burden to show it did not produce the product that caused the harm. If a manufacturer cannot prove they did not cause it, then the market share rule applies.

    3. Factual Causation and Uncertainty: in some cases, there might be scientific uncertainty as to the cause of the plaintiff's injury. Environmental or other factors might

have contributed to the plaintiff's injury. In such cases, expert testimony is often used to establish factual connection, and the causation element might boil down to a battle of the experts.

C. Legal causation: also know as proximate causation, this part of causation requires the plaintiff to show that the injury is not the remote consequences of defendant's unreasonable conduct. Courts use two tests to analyze legal causation: the directness test and the foreseeability test.

1. Directness test: if the injury can be directly connected to the unreasonable conduct without an unforeseeable, intervening cause, then the unreasonable conduct is the legal cause of the injury. An unforeseeable, intervening cause is called superseding because it cuts off liability for the defendant.

2. Foreseeability test: if the injury is the foreseeable consequence of the unreasonable conduct, then the unreasonable conduct is the legal cause of the injury. The foreseeability test cuts off liability for injury that is not the predictable consequence of the unreasonable conduct. An important exception to the foreseeability test is the egg shell plaintiff rule: the defendant is liable for all personal injuries that are the direct and factual result of the unreasonable conduct even if the injury was not foreseeable. In other words, the defendant "is liable for the plaintiff as he finds him."

3. Legal policy: causation tends to be the most difficult part of the negligence claim. Courts sometimes become confused themselves. The best way to keep these issues clear is to work through the factual and legal causation parts systematically and run each causation issue through these various tests. Keep in mind, however, the overriding policy concern with holding a defendant liable for risky situations that are created by the defendant's unreasonable conduct.

CHAPTER 6

Negligence: Recoverable Damages

GENERAL APPROACH

Remember that the claim for negligence has four elements: duty, breach, causation, and damages. We have discussed the first three; this chapter discusses the fourth and last element: damages. In order to establish negligence, a plaintiff must show that there were damages suffered. Damages are the legal injuries that can be the basis for compensation. Notice in Chapter Eight, we will discuss the topic of "Tort Remedies." Chapter Eight deals with the full set of remedies that a court can award to a successful plaintiff. These remedies include compensatory and punitive damages. In this chapter, we focus on the damages that the plaintiff must prove in order to establish the claim of negligence. The damages the plaintiff proves will be the basis for a court to determine the award of compensatory damages, which we will discuss in greater detail in Chapter Eight.

This chapter is divided into two sections. The first deals with survival and wrongful death actions, a legal mechanism for relatives of a tort victim to recover damages. The second deals with the types of recoverable damages a plaintiff has to show in order to establish the fourth element of negligence.

SURVIVAL AND WRONGFUL DEATH ACTIONS

Your Torts class will mention briefly survival and wrongful death actions. All states have created these actions by statute. These statutes were enacted to reverse a harsh common law rule which held that all tort claims dies with the victim. In other words, if a victim of a tort died, then no one could bring a tort claim against the tortfeasor.

A survival action allows the estate of the decedent to bring tort claims on behalf of the deceased. The executor of the estate, or sometimes a designated heir, can step in the shoes of the deceased and bring the relevant tort claim as the plaintiff. The party bringing the claim has all the obligations to prove the claim that the deceased party would have had if the claim had been brought directly. A survival statute does place some limitations on what damages are recoverable, however. For example, pain and suffering is often limited in a survival action for the simple reason that the decedent is not in a position to experience future pain and suffering, However, the pain and suffering experienced by the decedent before death is often recoverable.

A wrongful death action allows a survivor to bring a suit for the wrongful death of the tort victim. This action allows the survivor to recover damages for injuries that the survivor has experienced as a result of the death of the tort victim. Only a certain set of survivors can bring the suit. They are limited in most instances to the legal spouse and children, by statute. The survivor bringing the suit will raise the relevant tort claims against the tortfeasor and is subject to the same defenses that the tortfeasor would have had against the deceased tort victim. We will discuss these defenses in greater detail in Chapter Nine. A wrongful death statute will sometimes limit the types of damages that can be recovered, but they usually include loss of economic support, loss of consortium, and economic injuries that resulted from the wrongful death.

TYPES OF RECOVERABLE DAMAGES

There are two categories of recoverable damages: pecuniary and non-pecuniary. Pecuniary damages are also called special damages and non-pecuniary damages, general damages.

Pecuniary damages are out-of-pocket monetary damages that were caused by the defendant's breach of duty to exercise reasonable care. They include items like medical expenses, lost wages, and property damage. Remember from our discussion of duty in Chapter Three that pure economic loss is not recoverable unless there is a physical impact. A plaintiff has to show pecuniary damages with specificity and often will require receipts or some objective basis for determining their amount.

Non-pecuniary damages are the non-monetary damages that were caused by the defendant's breach of duty to exercise reasonable care. They include items like pain and suffering, loss of enjoyment of life (also known as hedonic damages), and loss of consortium. Keep in mind the limitations on recovery for pure emotional loss discussed in Chapter Three. Even though these types of damages are described as non-monetary, the court must place a dollar amount on these injuries. A jury is instructed to award what a "reasonable person would award" to compensate for these injuries. A judge has discretion to lower or, in state cases only, to increase the jury award if the amount is deemed unreasonable. As you can imagine, there is controversy over the setting of the award for non-pecuniary damages, and we will discuss in Chapter Eight, statutory measures to place caps on non-pecuniary damages.

Some jurisdictions do not allow separate recovery for hedonic damages from recovery for pain and suffering; other jurisdictions do. Most jurisdictions have some limits on loss of consortium, or the emotional loss suffered by a spouse, child or parent from the loss of companionship arising from either the death or injury of the tort victim. A loss of consortium claim can be raised by the legal spouse or child of a tort victim. Some jurisdictions, however, limit when a parent can bring a loss of consortium claim.

■ PROBLEMS ■

1. Defendant runs a day care center that includes an indoor play and recreation room and an outdoor playground that includes a swing set and a slide. The center is licensed by the state and complies with all applicable regulations. One day A and B, both five years old, are playing on the swing set when a stray dog enters the

playground and bites B before running away. The playground is open and not fenced in. Several other children (all the way from C to Z) have been bitten by a stray dog in the playground before. Defendant cleans B's wound and places a bandage over the bite, but does not take B to the hospital. Instead, when B's parent picks up B at the end of the day, Defendant informs B's parent about the incident. B is immediately taken to the hospital where he is examined. The doctor finds that there is some chance of rabies and gives B a series of shots to deal with the potential disease. B's parent has to pay $4000 in hospital bills and has to miss three days of work to take care of B. In addition, B has developed a fear of the family dog, who must be given away, and B develops emotional distress at the thought of the bite and the shots, which manifests itself in loss of sleep and occasional and unexpected nausea. B's parent and B sue Defendant for negligence, claiming that Defendant's unreasonable conduct resulted in the dog bite, the hospital expenses, and B's trauma. The jurisdiction has adopted a statute governing punitive damages which (1) requires a bifurcated trial, (2) caps punitive damages at 3 times pecuniary damages, (3) allows punitive damages only when Defendant has acted recklessly or intentionally, and (4) allows punitive damages to be based solely on the factors in *BMW v. Gore*. Identify the pecuniary and non-pecuniary damages claimed under these facts. What arguments does Defendant have against recovery?

Suggested Answers

1. Let us divide up the damages into those claimed by the parents and those claimed by B. In analyzing these damages, keep in mind that pecuniary damages are those that compensate for out of pocket expenses and non-pecuniary damages are those compensate for pain and suffering and emotional damages.

Here, B's damages are non-pecuniary. They would include the emotional distress from the shots, the emotional trauma of the accident, the physical injuries and the fear of the dog. Plaintiff most likely would plead all of these as pain and suffering. Defendant, however, will try to rebut some of the elements of damages.

First, Defendant will try to rebut several aspects of these damages on causation grounds, trying to argue either that there is no causal connection between the breach of duty and the damages or that the causal connection is too remote for recovery. This argument might work for the fear of the dog and the emotional trauma of the accident if the Defendant can show that these damages were independent of the accident. Perhaps, B never got along with dogs before the accident or had suffered this emotional trauma before the accident. Note, however, that if B had a nervous condition that made her particularly susceptible to the accident, Defendant has to take the plaintiff as is, so to speak, under the eggshell skull rule.

Second, Defendant may argue against recovery for emotional damage based on negligence. Some courts are skeptical about negligent infliction of emotional distress claims. Some courts conclude that recovery for emotional distress is available if there is breach of some independent duty. Here, B has claims for physical injuries, the dog bite and the treatment at the hospital. Which are recoverable under the negligence claim. Recovery for emotional distress can be recovered if they arise from the physical injury. This last point is an issue of causation discussed in the previous paragraph.

B's parents' damages are for the hospital bills and the lost days of work. These are pecuniary damages, and Defendant can argue against them based upon the amount and the causal connection. The issue of amount is exclusively a factual question, and Defendant will have a hard time rebutting a hospital bill for the care of B unless the bill contains items that are unrelated to the treatment or are exorbitant. The lost days of work may raise some room for argument, however, based on causation. Defendant may argue that B's parents could have avoided those damages by reshifting hours and hiring a caregiver. The costs of hiring a caregiver would be compensable. Most likely, the damages for the lost days of work might be reduced to reflect the costs of providing B with care.

B's parents will also be able to raise claims for pain and suffering as non-pecuniary damages. There may be a problem with claims for emotional distress since there was no physical injury to the parents here. Furthermore, the parents cannot recover as bystanders since they were not present when the child was bitten by the dog. The parents probably will not be able to recover for loss of consortium since those claims are limited in some jurisdictions in cases where the child is not killed.

 ## CHECKLIST FOR NEGLIGENCE: RECOVERABLE DAMAGES

A. Damages is the fourth element of claim for negligence. A plaintiff must show that a defendant's unreasonable conduct resulted in damages.

B. Survival and wrongful death actions are mechanisms that allow the estate or a surviving relative of a tort victim to bring claims after the tort victim has died.

C. Categories of recoverable damages include pecuniary and non-pecuniary damages. Pecuniary damages are monetary injuries, such as medical bills, property damage, and lost wages. Non-pecuniary damages are pain and suffering, loss of enjoyment of life, and loss of consortium.

CHAPTER 7

Strict Liability

GENERAL APPROACH

Remember from the Introduction that there are three standards of care for tort liability: intent, negligence, and strict liability. We have discussed the first two; this chapter focuses on the third. Strict liability is liability without fault. Put simply, strict liability means that if a defendant has caused injury to a plaintiff, then the defendant is liable to the plaintiff regardless of intent or the unreasonableness of the defendant's conduct. An easy way to remember strict liability is by the phrase: "You broke it, you bought it." Courts in the United States have shied away from imposing strict liability because of its potential adverse affect on risk-taking. If a person knows that they will be liable for harm even if they acted as reasonably as possible, the person may decide not to act at all, Consequently, courts have impose strict liability only in situations where the seriousness of the risk mandates making the defendant liable for the potential harm imposed on the plaintiff. There are three situations where strict liability is imposed: injury from wild animals owned by or in the possession of the defendant, abnormally dangerous activities undertaken by the defendant, and products liability. This chapter will focus on the first two, and Chapter Eleven will focus on products liability.

Most courts emphasize that strict liability does not mean absolute liability. First of all, the defendant can raise defenses to strict liability, many of which overlap with the defenses that arise under negligence. We discuss these defenses in Chapter Nine.

Second, the plaintiff has the burden to establish a strict liability. The elements of strict liability are duty, breach, causation, and damages. They sound very much like the elements of a negligence claim, but there are two important differences. Duty under strict liability arises only in three situations: (i) the duty to prevent harm from wild animals that one owns or possesses; (ii) the duty to prevent harm from abnormally dangerous activities that one engages in; and (iii) the duty to prevent harm from defects in products that one manufactures or sells. The breach element does not require the plaintiff to show that the defendant engaged in unreasonable conduct. In a strict liability claim, a plaintiff shows breach if the defendant has not fulfilled one of these three duties. The causation and damage elements of a strict liability are identical to the causation and damage elements of a negligence claim. For the rest of this chapter, we will explain these duties in greater detail.

ANIMALS

The owner or possessor of a wild animal is strictly liable for harms caused by that animal. This rule does not in general apply to domesticated animals, such as typical pets or farm animals, unless there is a known dangerous tendency of a particular animal. If a domesticated animal displays a dangerous tendency that is not known, liability for the harm is based on negligence, but not strict liability. This rule is sometimes, in the common parlance, is referred to as the one bite rule. What counts as a wild animal depends upon the circumstances and typically includes animals that are not normally kept as pets or on farms.

Your Torts class might cover the difference between "fence-in" and "fence-out" rules. Some jurisdictions put the burden on the landowner to fence out domesticated animals while other jurisdictions put the burden on the owner of the animal to fence them in. The difference between these jurisdictions is the placement of legal liability from animals that trespass on land and cause damage to property. In fence-out jurisdictions, the burden is on the landowner to put up a fence, and failure to put up a fence places liability on the landowner for harm to his property. In fence-in jurisdictions, the burden is on the animal owner to fence in the animal, and failure to put up a fence places liability on the animal owner for harm to the property of another. In both jurisdictions, if the appropriate party did have a fence, then liability is based on negligence rather than on strict liability.

ABNORMALLY DANGEROUS ACTIVITIES

Strict liability for abnormally dangerous activities can be traced back to the English case of *Rylands v. Fletcher*, UKHL 1 (1868), a decision that has been largely rejected in the United States. Despite the hostility to the decision in the United States, the decision is an important one for establishing a rule for strict liability whose spirit is recognized in some aspects of U.S. tort law even if the letter is not followed exactly. The rule, sometimes called the "escape principle," goes as follows:

> [the person who for his own purposes brings on his lands and collects and keeps there anything likely to do mischief if it escapes, must keep it in at his own peril and . . . is prima facie answerable for all the damages which is the natural consequence of its escape. Id.]

The "escape principle" has largely been rejected in the United States as a general basis for establishing strict liability. Instead, United States courts recognized it in particular applications. The principle provided the basis for strict liability for wild animals. The principle also provided the basis for liability for abnormally dangerous activities.

Early on, liability for abnormally dangerous activities was known as liability for ultrahazardous activities, and that phrase still appears in the case law. Courts applied strict liability on a case by case basis and imposed it in such activities as blasting, ballooning, and transporting flammable substances on the highway. Overtime courts developed a multi-factor test for determining when an activity is deemed ultrahazardous. The Restatement (Second) of Torts summarized these factors in Section 520 under the label "abnormally dangerous activities," which is the common term now that you should use.

Section 520 lists the following six factors to determine when an activity is abnormally hazardous resulting in strict liability for any harm that results from the activity. They can be summarized as follows:

(i)   high degree of risk to person or property;

(ii) chance of great harm;

(iii) risk cannot be eliminated with reasonable care;

(iv) activity is not a matter of common usage;

(v)   inappropriateness of activity to place carried on;

(vi) dangers of activity outweigh its value to the community.

Courts have criticized these factors and have attempted to simplify the test. The Restatement (Third) of Torts, in Section 20, recommends a simplified version of the test based on factors (iii) and (iv):

(i)   activity creates a foreseeable and highly significant risk even with reasonable care;

(ii) activity not a matter of common usage.

When dealing with an issue of what constitutes an abnormally dangerous activity, work through each test depending on what is covered in your particular Torts class. The main controversy with the Second Restatement test arises from its factor (v), the inappropriateness of activity to place carried on. Courts reasoned that potential defendants might escape liability under (v) by simply relocating activities to remote areas even though a risk still might be imposed to society. For example, blasting or storing hazardous substances in remote areas might still pose a risk to society, especially as neighborhoods expand and new construction takes place. The Third Restatement factors summarize the factors that have been important in how courts have determined whether an activity is abnormally dangerous.

PRODUCTS LIABILITY

A manufacturer, distributor, or seller of a defective product is strictly liable to the purchaser, user, or third parties harmed by the product. We will discuss products liability in greater detail in Chapter Eleven, but it is important to recognize the duty here as one of the three major areas where strict liability applies in the United States.

■ PROBLEMS ■

1. Chemical Company shipped a highly flammable and toxic chemical from its factory in State A to a plant in State B. The Company hired a Shipping Company that used a railcar to transport the chemical to the plant. Just outside the plant in State B, the railcar containing the chemical fell off the tracks, causing the chemical to spill into drinking water requiring great cost of cleanup. In addition, several homeowners were injured by the chemicals when it contaminated the drinking water. The homeowners want to bring a claim of strict liability against (a) the manufacturer of the rail car, (b) Shipping Company, and (c) Chemical Company.

Suggested Answers

1. (a) In answering this question, apply the six factor test under Restatement Second Section 520, starting with the third factor, the inability to avoid the risk by the exercise of reasonable care. The remaining five factors are the severity of the risk, the gravity of the harm, the extent to which activity is manner of common usage, the inappropriateness of the activity to the place where it is carried out, and the comparison of the value to the community and the dangerous attributes of the activity. Here, manufacturing of the rail

car could occur with reasonable care. The argument that the plaintiff might have, however, is that rail cars used to transport hazardous chemicals cannot be manufactured solely with reasonable care; extraordinary care is required. Plaintiff might argue that specially designed cars could have been made to keep the chemicals from spilling, in light of the probability that the car could spill and the risks resulting from the spill. The problem is that the remaining three factors may work against Plaintiff. Manufacturing railcars for multiple uses is a common activity, and there does not seem to be anything inappropriate to the railcar being used in this neighborhood, if used carefully. Furthermore, the value of creating special railcars may outweigh the risks, especially if reasonable care can avoid the risk. Most likely, the plaintiffs will have to proceed on a negligence claim rather than a strict liability claim.

(b) The plaintiffs will try to argue that the shipping of dangerous chemicals, especially near drinking water that serves residential areas, is an abnormally dangerous activity mandating strict liability. Focusing the six factor test, however, the third factor militates against strict liability because the activity of shipping can be pursued through reasonable conduct. Turning to some of the other factors, the severity of the risk, the gravity of the harm, the extent to which the activity is a manner of common usage, and the inappropriateness of the activity to the place where it is carried out, these all seem to weigh in favor of strict liability given the dangers involved. The final factor, the comparison of the value to the community and the dangerous attributes of the activity, may go either way since there is economic value from having shipping and railways in the community. There are some arguments in favor of strict liability, but given that the activity can be conducted with reasonable care, the plaintiffs do have a negligence claim here and strict liability may not be warranted.

(c) The case for strict liability against Chemical Company may not be very strong. The Company was not involved in the shipping of the chemical. It had contracted with another company to undertake that activity, as discussed in (b). The decision to hire the shipper is a question of reasonableness, rather than a decision for which Chemical Company would be strictly liable. Furthermore, products liability would not be applicable here because there is no suggestion that the chemical at issue was defective.

CHECKLIST FOR STRICT LIABILITY ✔

A. Strict liability is the third standard of care for tort liability. Strict liability imposes liability for harm caused by a defendant regardless of intent or unreasonable conduct.

B. To establish a claim for strict liability, a plaintiff has to establish duty, breach, causation and damages.

   1. For strict liability claims, duty arises in three instances:

      (a) duty to prevent harm from wild animals one owns or possesses;

      (b) duty to prevent harm from abnormally dangerous activities;

      (c) duty to prevent harm from defective products.

   2. The breach element of strict liability does not require the plaintiff to establish that the defendant acted unreasonably. For strict liability, breach requires the plaintiff to establish that the defendant failed to carry out one of the three duties defendant had under strict liability.

   3. The elements of causation and damages under strict liability are similar to those under negligence.

C. Special rules to remember about strict liability:

   1. Strict liability for wild animals may also apply to domestic animals with known dangerous tendencies.

   2. Courts use a multifactor test in determining whether an activity is abnormally dangerous.

   3. The duty to prevent harm from defective products applies to manufacturers, distributors, and sellers of the product.

CHAPTER 8

Tort Remedies

GENERAL APPROACH

Once a plaintiff has proven a tort claim against a defendant, the court will provide a remedy for the plaintiff's injuries. A general principle of remedies is that a plaintiff can recover once for each injury suffered. Keep in mind, however, that a plaintiff can raise multiple claims against a defendant in the hopes of winning on one of them. Suppose a defendant has run into a plaintiff with a car. The plaintiff can claim that defendant did so intentionally and, alternatively, that the defendant did so negligently. But the plaintiff can recover only once for all the injuries that resulted from being hit by the defendant. Therefore, the three forms of tort liability, intentional, negligent, and strict, are legal bases for recovery from the defendant. But regardless of whichever legal basis the plaintiff is able to establish, the tort remedy will be designed along the legal rules presented in this chapter.

There are two types of tort remedies: injunctions and damages. Damages are divided into two types: compensatory and punitive. Damages are the more common type of remedies in tort law because of the goals of compensation and deterrence. Your course may discuss insurance law issues. We will touch on insurance very briefly here. But think of insurance as a source of money to finance the damages that a plaintiff is entitled to. The basic rules about damages apply whether the plaintiff sues the defendant or his insurance company or if the plaintiff's insurance company sues the defendant in the shoes of the plaintiff.

INJUNCTIONS

An injunction is a remedy imposed by the court ordering the defendant to affirmatively do something or to refrain from doing something. In the area of tort law, injunctive relief is rare except for the intentional tort of trespass to land and for some advanced areas, such as products liability, defamation, or business torts. For example, in a products liability case, a court might order a company to recall a product that has been found defective from the marketplace. In a defamation case, as another example, a court may order a newspaper to publish a correction to an article that contained false and defamatory information. Finally, in a business tort case, a court may order a company not to use a trade secret or other proprietary information that had been misappropriated from a competitor. We will discuss these more advanced examples in Chapters Eleven through Thirteen. In the more basic personal and economic injury tort cases, the remedy of an injunction does not make much sense because the court is trying to compensate a plaintiff for harm that was caused by the defendant. Damages, therefore, are the more appropriate remedy.

DAMAGES

Damages are an award of money that the defendant must pay to the plaintiff as a remedy for a tort claim. There are two types of damages that a court will award: compensatory and punitive. As the names suggest, compensatory damages are set to compensate the plaintiff for the injury suffered while punitive damages are set to punish the defendant and deter future improper conduct.

Compensatory Damages

Compensatory damages are an award of money calculated to put the plaintiff in the position he would have been had the tort not occurred. This definition is abstract because it is based on a hypothetical notion of the accident not having occurred. In practice, compensatory damages are related to the damages that have to be shown to make a claim of negligence or strict liability discussed in Chapters Six and Seven. For intentional tort claims, compensatory damages are based on the nature of the intentional tort. For example, if the intentional tort claim is a battery, compensatory damages will be set to compensate for the physical harm caused by the defendant's touching. If the intentional tort claim is based on harm to property, then compensatory damages will be based on the injury to property. Similarly, if the intentional tort claim is based on mental harms, compensatory damages will be based on the costs of these mental harms.

Compensatory damages will be calculated based on objective evidence introduced by the parties. For example, if injuries include property damage or economic harm, courts will look at out of pocket expenses, such as the cost of repair, to calculate the amount of compensatory damages. Physical and mental injuries can be measure by hospital and doctor bills. Recovery for emotional loss, such as pain and suffering, will often be based on the testimony of the injured party and will be based on what is reasonable in light of the nature of the injury.

Because of the less objective nature of emotional loss, many jurisdictions have imposed statutory caps on the amount of recovery for non-pecuniary losses, such as pain and suffering. A typical cap level is $200,000. These caps are controversial because they lead to inequitable results. Plaintiffs who own little property or who may not have very much in loss income will not obtain less than those plaintiffs who suffer greater property loss or have larger incomes. Some state supreme courts have struck down these statutory caps as being unconstitutional under the relevant state constitution. The courts struck down these caps as violating the plaintiff's right to a jury trial in which the jury determines the amount of compensatory damages. Statutory caps are an example of state level tort reform.

There are four issues that need to be highlighted about compensatory damages: (1) plaintiff's duty to mitigate, (2) prejudgment interest, (3) discounting, and (4) the collateral source rule.

1.   Plaintiff's Duty to Mitigate: A court will reduce the amount of compensatory damages if a plaintiff has failed to take reasonable steps to mitigate damages. For example, if the plaintiff has lost a job as a result of an accident, there is a duty to take reasonable steps to find alternative sources of income. Similarly, if the plaintiff has suffered property loss, such as loss of a vehicle, the plaintiff must take reasonable steps to replace the vehicle or find alternate means of transportation. Finally, if a plaintiff has suffered physical injury, the plaintiff needs to seek medical attention to ensure that the injuries do not become worse, resulting in unreasonable medical expenses.

2.   Prejudgment interest: Compensatory damages are designed to compensate the injured party for harm that occurred at the time of the accident. But there is often a long period between the accident and the time of a tort judgment when the remedy is imposed by the court. Because of this delay, courts can award prejudgment interest from the time of the accident to the time of judgment. Prejudgment interest is at the discretion of the trial court judge and is designed to compensate for the delay in litigation. Judges base the award of prejudgment interest on the amount of delay, the adequacy of the compensatory damage award, and the reason for the delay.

3.   Discounting: Compensatory damages often involve compensation for future losses. For example, an injured party may not be able to work anymore and therefore a component of the damages is lost future income. However, the judgment is made against the defendant at a particular point in time. Therefore, the amount awarded for future losses must take into consideration that the value of money is different over time. Courts account for the time value of money through a method called discounting. For example, a plaintiff's lost income might be $100,000 per year for 10 years into the future. If the court awarded the plaintiff one

million dollars today (that is the $100,000 times 10), then the plaintiff will be overcompensated for the lost income. Why? Because the plaintiff could take the one million dollars awarded today and earn interest on that amount over ten years and get back more than what was actually lost. Therefore, the court will award something less than the million dollars (a discount based on an estimate of the interest rate and inflation), to give to the plaintiff a more accurate measure of the lost income that has been actually lost. There are other financial ways to deal with this issue of the time value of money, such as annuities and structured settlements, but those are topics that go beyond the basic Torts class. The concept of discounting, however, is one that you should be at least familiar with since it is a quite common practice in determining compensatory damages.

4.   Collateral Source Rule: Often, a plaintiff may have alternative sources of recovery for the injuries suffered. For example, a plaintiff may draw down on savings, obtain gifts or loans from friends and family, or have an insurance claim that compensates for some of the personal or property injury. Under the collateral source rule, these alternative sources of compensation cannot be used to reduce the amount of a compensatory damages award. There are two rationales for the collateral source rule. The first is that a defendant should not benefit from the fact the plaintiff was prudent in buying insurance or had other sources of compensation, such as friends or family. The collateral source rule supports the deterrence function of tort law. The second common explanation for the rule is to not discourage people from buying insurance or accepting gifts or loans on the grounds that such payments will lower the award of compensatory damages. The tort system, in other words, is not meant to be the only source of compensation, The obvious problem with the collateral source rule is that it leads to double recovery for the plaintiff which may be viewed as unfair. Some jurisdictions have limited the collateral source rule in limited cases, such as with respect to settlements from multiple defendants (a point we will talk about in Chapter Nine under the issue of apportionment of damages) or government insurance, such as worker's compensation.

Punitive Damages

Punitive damages are an amount of money awarded to a
plaintiff to deter malicious or grossly reckless conduct by a
defendant. One of the justifications for punitive damages is
deterrence. Another justification is sometimes referred to as
"supercompensatory." This second justification reflects the view
that compensatory damages may not adequately measure the full
amount of harm suffered by the plaintiff. Punitive damages are
sometimes referred to as exemplary damages by some state courts.

Punitive damages are reserved for cases in which the defendant's conduct rises beyond the traditional standards of intent or
negligence. In order to recover punitive damages, a plaintiff has to
establish that a defendant has acted with malice or with gross
recklessness. Once the plaintiff has shown these extra elements of
the defendant's misconduct, then a jury determines the amount of
punitive damages. The judge will then award punitive damages on
top of the compensatory damages as a judgment against the
defendant.

Because of a concern with runaway jury awards and unfairness to defendants, punitive damage awards have come under legal
scrutiny both at the federal and state levels. The two issues you
need to be aware of are: (1) limitation on punitive damage awards
under the Due Process Clause of the United States Constitution
and (2) limitation on punitive damages under state law that have
been implemented as part of tort reform.

1.   The Due Process Clause of the United States Constitution:
In 1996, the United States Supreme Court ruled in *BMW v. Gore*,
517 U.S. 559 (1996), that a punitive damage award violates the U.S.
Constitution if it is "grossly excessive." To determine whether a
punitive damage award is grossly excessive, a judge must look to
three factors: (i) the reprehensibility of the defendant's conduct; (ii)
the ratio of the punitive damage award to the compensatory award
in the particular case; and (iii) the comparison of the punitive
damage award with criminal or other sanctions for similar conduct.
All three factors need to be considered and given equal weight in
determining the excessiveness of a punitive damage award. If an

award is found to be excessive, then the judge can strike it down and have a jury determine the amount of the award again.

Subsequent cases have attempted to clarify the three factor test in *BMW v. Gore*. In *State Farm v. Campbell*, 538 U.S. 408 (2003), the U.S. Supreme Court held that, in general, single digit ratios between punitive and compensatory damages are not grossly excessive, but double digit ratios and higher are suspect. The Court in *Campbell* also presented four factors that should be considered in determining whether a defendant's conduct is reprehensible: (i) physical harm makes conduct more reprehensible, (ii) indifference or tortious disregard on the part of the defendant makes conduct more reprehensible, (iii) repeated conduct by the defendant makes conduct more reprehensible, and (iv) malicious action makes the conduct more reprehensible. Finally, in *Philip Morris USA v. Williams*, 549 U.S. 346 (2007), the Court ruled that a punitive damage award could not be based on injuries suffered by parties not party to the litigation.

2.   State law limitations on punitive damages: Many states have passed statutes that impose limitations on punitive damage awards. There are many variations on tort reform of punitive damages. There are four reforms that are common across states: (i) the requirement of bifurcated trials; (ii) the decoupling of punitive and compensatory damages; (iii) the enumeration of factors that are acceptable for a jury to consider in determining punitive damages; and (iv) caps on punitive damages.

The requirement of bifurcated trials means that a different jury must be empanelled to determine the amount of punitive damages from the jury that determined liability. The justification for this requirement is to separate the determination of the amount of punitive damages from the determination of liability. The concern is that evidence about liability might taint the jury's judgment in setting the amount of the damages.

The decoupling requirement means that the plaintiff does not keep the full amount of the punitive damage award. The justification is that the plaintiff receives a windfall beyond compensation from a large punitive damage award. Furthermore, there is the concern that jurors might be swayed by a particularly sympathetic plaintiff in increasing the size of the award. States that have implemented decoupling require that a certain percentage of the punitive damage award goes to the state to implement programs to compensate other victims or to remedy the harms from the tort more broadly.

In response to concerns that juries determine punitive damages on irrational factors, many states enumerate a list of factors that are designed to guide the jury in setting punitive damage awards consistently with the policies of tort law. The list of factors varies from state to state but typically includes factors like the magnitude of the harm, the number of victims, the extent to which the defendant profited from the tort, and the economic condition of the defendant.

Finally, some states have implemented caps on punitive damages. These caps are often set as multiples usually using pecuniary damages as the baseline. Caps on punitive damages have usually been upheld by state supreme courts unlike caps on non-pecuniary damages which are found to violate the plaintiff's right to a jury trial. Caps on punitive damages are often understood as necessary to protect the due process rights of the defendant.

■ PROBLEMS ■

---

1.   Defendant runs a day care center that includes an indoor play and recreation room and an outdoor playground that includes a swing set and a slide. The center is licensed by the state and complies with all applicable regulations. One day A and B, both five years old, are playing on the swing set when a stray dog enters the playground and bites B before running away. The playground is open and not fenced in. Several other children (all the way from C to Z) have been bitten by a stray dog in the playground before. Defendant cleans B's wound and places a bandage over the bite, but does not take B to the hospital. Instead, when B's parent picks up B at the end of the day, Defendant informs B's parent about the

incident. B is immediately taken to the hospital where he is examined. The doctor finds that there is some chance of rabies and gives B a series of shots to deal with the potential disease. B's parent has to pay $4000 in hospital bills and has to miss three days of work to take care of B. In addition, B has developed a fear of the family dog, who must be given away, and B develops emotional distress at the thought of the bite and the shots, which manifests itself in loss of sleep and occasional and unexpected nausea. B's parent and B sue Defendant for negligence, claiming that Defendant's unreasonable conduct resulted in the dog bite, the hospital expenses, and B's trauma. The jurisdiction has adopted a statute governing punitive damages which (1) requires a bifurcated trial, (2) caps punitive damages at 3 times pecuniary damages, (3) allows punitive damages only when Defendant has acted recklessly or intentionally, and (4) allows punitive damages to be based solely on the factors in *BMW v. Gore*. Suppose the jury returns a damage award of $10,000 compensatory and $500,000 punitive. Analyze.

Suggested Answers

1.   There are several problems with the jury's punitive damage awards under the relevant state statute. First, the state requires a bifurcated trial to determine the amount of punitive damages. Here, the same jury determined liability, compensatory damages, and punitive damages. That is clear error and would be grounds for reversal. Second, the state caps punitive damages at 3 times pecuniary damages. Here, punitive damages were found to be 50 times the total amount of compensatory damages, which consists of pecuniary and non-pecuniary damages. Third, there has to be a finding that Defendant acted intentionally or recklessly in order to award punitive damages. Here, intent may be difficult to prove since there is no evidence of deliberateness or of knowledge with substantial certainty, but recklessness might be a possibility if Defendant imposed a serious or substantial risk, beyond negligence, in exposing children to potential dog bites and B to the possibility of contracting rabies. Finally, the state statute incorporates the *BMW v. Gore* standard. Under *BMW v. Gore*, the amount

of punitive damages should reflect the reprehensibility of the conduct, the relationship to the amount of harm or potential harm suffered by plaintiff, and any available civil penalty in comparable cases. Defendant might argue that the conduct is not reprehensible and that the award is grossly excessive in light of the actual harm suffered by plaintiffs. Furthermore, Defendant might also point to comparable penalties for endangering children or for poorly maintaining a child care facility in order to put the punitive damage award in perspective. As for reprehensibility, Plaintiff might point to the number of similar incidents that had taken place at the facility. But Plaintiff needs to be careful that the amount of punitive damages is not based on the number of other accidents, in light of the *Philip Morris* case.

✓ CHECKLIST FOR TORT REMEDIES

A. After a plaintiff has established a tort claim against a defendant, the court will award the plaintiff a remedy for the injuries suffered. Although a plaintiff might have multiple claims for the same injury, there can be only one remedy for the injury suffered.

B. Injunctions are one type of remedy. They are a court order telling the defendant to do something or to refrain from doing something. Injunctions are often used as a remedy for trespass to land and for more advanced tort claims based on products liability, defamation, or business torts.

C. Damages are another type of remedy and the preferred type in most tort cases. Damages are an award of money to the plaintiff as a remedy for a tort claim. There are two types: compensatory and punitive.

    1. Compensatory damages are an amount of money calculated to compensate the plaintiff for the injury suffered. The plaintiff must prove the amount of compensatory damages. Some states have imposed caps on the non-pecuniary aspect of compensatory damages.

        a. Plaintiff has a duty to mitigate damages.

b. A judge has discretion to award prejudgment interest.

c. A judge will discount damages for future losses.

d. The collateral source rule states that compensatory damages will not be reduced by the amount of compensation that the plaintiff has received from other sources, such as insurance.

2. Punitive damages are an amount of money calculated to punish the defendant for malicious or grossly reckless conduct.

a. Punitive damages cannot be grossly excessive or they violate the Due Process Clause of the U.S. Constitution.

(i) Grossly excessive is determined by considering (a) the reprehensibility of the conduct, (b) the ratio of punitive to compensatory damages, and (c) the comparison to sanctions for similar conduct under criminal or other law.

(ii) In general, single digit ratios of punitive to compensatory damages are not grossly excessive.

(iii) Reprehensibility is determined by (a) physical injury, (b) indifference or disregard of defendant, (c) repeated action by defendant, and (d) intent or malice of defendant.

(iv) Injuries to parties not represented in the litigation cannot be a basis to determine the amount of punitive damages.

b. States have enacted various limitations of punitive damages. Such limitations include:

(i) Bifurcated trials.

(ii) Decoupling of punitive and compensatory damages.

(iii) Enumeration of factors for determining punitive damages.

(iv) Caps on punitive damages expressed as multiples of pecuniary damages.

CHAPTER 9

Defenses to Negligence and Strict Liability Claims

GENERAL APPROACH

A defendant has several defenses against a plaintiff's negligence and strict liability claims. These defenses can be broken down into two categories: defenses based on the plaintiff's conduct and defenses based on the defendant's status. Defenses based on the plaintiff's conduct rest on the argument that the plaintiff either assumed the risk posed by defendant's conduct or that plaintiff's unreasonable conduct also caused or contributed to the injury. Defenses based on the defendant's status rest on special rules that exempt certain actors from tort liability. This second set of defenses includes immunities for charities, immunities for members of a family, and immunities for state entities and actors.

DEFENSES BASED ON THE PLAINTIFF'S CONDUCT

A defendant can point to plaintiff's conduct as a defense to a negligence or strict liability claim. There are three defenses that can be used based on plaintiff's conduct: (i) assumption of risk; (ii) contributory negligence; and (iii) comparative negligence.

Assumption of Risk

The defense of assumption of risk rests on the argument that the plaintiff was aware of the risk posed by the defendant and voluntarily accepted it. Because of the plaintiff's consent to the risk, the plaintiff cannot recover the injury that resulted from a known, voluntarily accepted risk. There are three types of assumption of risk defenses; defendant has to establish only one of them to escape liability for a negligence or strict liability claim. The three types are: (i) express assumption of risk; (ii) primary assumption of risk; and (iii) secondary, or implied, assumption of risk.

<u>Express Assumption of Risk</u>

Express assumption of risk is based in contract law. The plaintiff contractually accepted the risks associated with the defendant's conduct or has voluntarily exculpated the defendant from liability. Often, express assumption of risk is associated with an exculpatory clause, a term of a contract that waives any legal claims against the defendant. Because of the concerns arising from unequal bargaining power in setting contractual terms, courts have been concerned that express assumption of risk and exculpatory clauses might violate the public policy of compensation and deterrence. The California Supreme Court addressed these public policy concerns in *Tunkl v. Regents of the Univ. of Cal.*, 60 Cal. 2d 92 (Cal. 1963). In this decision, the court laid our six factors to use to determine when express assumption of risk violates public policy. These so-called *Tunkl* factors are widely influential and have been adopted by most other states.

The *Tunkl* factors are: (i) the defendant is in a business that is thought suitable for public regulation; (ii) the defendant is performing a service of great importance to the public, which is often a matter of practical necessity for some members of the public; (iii) the defendant holds himself out as willing to perform the service for any member of the public who seeks it; (iv) because of the necessity of the service provided, the defendant has a bargaining advantage against members of the public who seek the service; (v) the defendant seeks exculpation through a standard adhesion contract and does not provide the option of obtaining protection against injury by paying additional fees; and (vi) the defendant in rendering service obtains control over the person or property of the person obtaining the service.

Express assumption of risk has been a difficult defense in such activities as medical care or child care. The hardest cases are sports activities which often entail risk of injury but are arguably not necessary for the participants. The policy rationale behind express assumption of risk is respecting the autonomy and voluntary choice of the plaintiff, but also not allowing the defendant to escape liability for risky activities when the plaintiff may not have any real choice in seeking a service from the defendant.

Primary Assumption of Risk

While express assumption of risk is contractual, primary assumption of risk is based on the inherent and known risks of an activity. Primary assumption of risk applies when there is no express contract that waived defendant's liability. Primary assumption of risk arises in sports or gaming activities. For example, sitting in the stands during a sporting event entails risks from balls flying into the audience. This risk is an example of one that would not give rise to liability because of primary assumption of risk. One has to be careful in applying this defense because the inherency of a risk will depend upon what are the rules of the game. For example, if many stadiums place a net or a shield around the audience to protect attendees from objects flying into the stands, then there may be an expectation for such safety devices in other venues. This expectation would militate against primary assumption of risk as a viable defense. In contrast, the risk of a player running into the stands and injuring an attendee is not part of the rules of the game, and therefore would not fall under primary assumption of risk.

The determination of primary assumption of risk rests on how the rules of the game associated with a particular activity are understood in society. This understanding is then reflected in the law. Be careful of circular or trivial versions of the argument in favor of primary assumption of risk. For example, surgery has inherent and known risks associated with it. But courts do not apply primary assumption of risk in this context because the expectation is that medical care providers will exercise due care in taking care of the patient. The risk of the medical procedure falls on the medical care provider, not on the patient.

In analyzing a problem, first look to see if there is a contractual basis for assumption of risk. If there is, then apply the *Tunkl* factors above to see if express assumption of risk would apply. If there is no contract, then look to see if the risk at issue in the problem is inherent and known to the activity based on the rules of the game, or expectations, associated with the activity. Primary assumption of risk is the defense based on these inherent and known risks.

Secondary, or Implied, Assumption of Risk

In situations where there is no express contract or the risk is not inherent in the activity, the defendant might rely on the defense of secondary, or implied, assumption of risk. Secondary assumption of risk applies when the plaintiff is told about a specific risk associated with an activity and voluntarily undertakes the activity anyway. The example that is often given of secondary assumption of risk is a plaintiff voluntarily and knowingly accepting a drive from a driver who is intoxicated. In this case, if the plaintiff knew that the drive was drunk but went with the driver anyway, then the driver, if sued later for negligence, can raise the defense of secondary assumption of risk against the plaintiff. Secondary assumption of risk is based in the notion of implied in fact contract. Although there is no express contract in the example of the drunk driver, there is an implicit exculpation of the defendant if the plaintiff knows about the risk and voluntarily undertakes the activity anyway. Another way to understand the defense of secondary assumption of risk is that it is based on unreasonable conduct of the plaintiff. Under this view, secondary assumption of risk is closer in policy to the defenses of contributory negligence and comparative negligence discussed next.

Contributory Negligence and Last Clear Chance

A defendant establishes the defense of contributory negligence by showing that the plaintiff's unreasonable conduct caused plaintiff's injuries. The defense of contributory negligence is "all or nothing," in the sense that if a plaintiff's unreasonable contributed to the injuries at all, then the plaintiff cannot recover. Under contributory negligence, there is no consideration of the relative contribution of the defendant's unreasonable conduct and the plaintiff's unreasonable conduct to the injuries and there is no consideration of who was more unreasonable. The policy behind the defense is that a plaintiff should not recover if the plaintiff had contributed through unreasonable conduct to the injury. Notice that this defense applies only to a negligence claim, but not a strict liability claim.

In establishing the defense of contributory negligence, a defendant has to show that the plaintiff's conduct was unreasonable and that the unreasonable conduct caused the injury. These elements are identical to a plaintiff's prima facie case for negligence. The types of evidence that a defendant would use to establish a plaintiff's unreasonable conduct are the same as what the plaintiff would use: custom, the Hand Formula, statutes, and special standards for children and the physically challenged. Furthermore, the causation analysis is also the same for the defendant as for the plaintiff's prima facie case.

There are two differences to note as well. First, *res ipsa loquitur* does not apply to the defense of contributory negligence. Remember *res ipsa loquitur* allows the plaintiff to use the accident itself as evidence of unreasonable conduct when no other evidence is available. Consequently, *res ipsa loquitur* is not relevant to proof of the defense, which arises only if the prima facie case has been established. Second, some courts are more favorable to the plaintiff on what constitutes unreasonable conduct especially when the plaintiff is a child or is physically challenged and the defendant is not. In this case of disparity between the plaintiff and the defendant, courts tend to require very strong evidence of unreasonableness to deny recovery to the plaintiff based on the contributory negligence defense.

In most jurisdictions, contributory negligence was found to be a harsh rule. Any unreasonable conduct on the part of the plaintiff that caused the injuries could deny any recovery for the plaintiff. As an example of such unfairness, consider the following example. A plaintiff is speeding in a car down a street. The speeding would be unreasonable conduct. A defendant truck driver is driving down the wrong side of the same street. This act would also be unreasonable. The two cars collide. The plaintiff would be denied recovery because of the defense of contributory negligence. Notice that in this example a truck has stuck a car with the plaintiff most likely suffering extensive damage. Arguably, however, the truck driver could have avoided the accident by simply switching to the correct side of the road. Courts addressed such unfairness of the contributory negligence doctrine by adopting the rule of last clear chance. If the plaintiff could show that the defendant had the last clear chance to avoid the accident, then the plaintiff could rebut the contributory negligence defense, and the defendant would be liable for negligence. The last clear chance would arise in situations where both the plaintiff and defendant were acting unreasonably, but the defendant had the last clear chance in the course of events to avoid the accident.

Comparative Negligence

Comparative negligence is a defense based on the unreasonable conduct of the plaintiff. Unlike contributory negligence, however, the defense requires the court, usually the jury, to compare the relative conduct of the defendants and the plaintiffs in the case. Under comparative negligence, the court will assign relative liability to the parties in the suit in percentage terms. Damages will be apportioned based on these percentages. For example, if there is one defendant and one plaintiff in the case, the court might find based on the evidence that defendant was 40% at fault and plaintiff was 60% at fault. These percentages would be used to allocate the damages to the plaintiff.

There are two rules for allocating damages. The first is the pure comparative negligence rule under which the percentages are used to reduce the amount a defendant to liable to a plaintiff. The second is the modified comparative negligence rule which reduces damages only if the defendant was found to more at fault than the plaintiff. Within modified comparative negligence states, there is a split in jurisdictions on how to treat cases where the plaintiff and the defendant were found to be equally at fault. Some jurisdictions give the tie to the plaintiff with the result that damages are reduced by the percentage of the defendant's fault. Other jurisdictions give the tie to the defendant with the result that the defendant is not liable at all. In the example above, a pure comparative negligence jurisdiction would award 40% of the damages to the plaintiff. A modified comparative negligence jurisdiction would award nothing to the plaintiff since the plaintiff was found to be more at fault than the defendant.

Comparative negligence is a defense that applies to both negligence and strict liability claims. Sometimes comparative negligence is referred to as comparative fault or comparative responsibility to reflect the fact that the court must determine relative liability of the plaintiff and defendant regardless of whether the strict liability or negligence of the defendant is at issue. Note that comparative negligence does not apply to intentional torts. No jurisdiction compares the relative fault of the plaintiff with the intentional act of the defendant. In other words, the negligence of the plaintiff is not a defense to an intentional tort claim. Furthermore, it is only the unreasonable conduct that becomes relevant in a comparative negligence regime. Even if the plaintiff was engaged in conduct that was intentional or would be subject to strict liability, the defendant has to show why that same conduct was unreasonable for the purpose of a comparative negligence defense.

Comparative negligence has been adopted by all jurisdictions in the United States except for Alabama, the District of Columbia, Maryland, North Carolina, and Virginia. States shifted to comparative negligence in the 1970s as a response to the unfairness of contributory negligence. The four states and the District that do not have comparative negligence still retain contributory negligence with last clear chance.

One important issue is the treatment of assumption of risk in states that have adopted comparative negligence. All states retain express assumption of risk as a defense under comparative negligence. Some states have gotten rid of secondary assumption of risk and subsumed it under the defense of the plaintiff's unreasonable conduct while retaining primary assumption of risk. Other states have gotten rid of both primary and secondary assumption of risk and subsumed both under the defense of the unreasonableness of the plaintiff. You should be aware of the different treatments of assumption of risk.

DEFENSES BASED ON THE DEFENDANT'S STATUS

A defendant can raise defenses to negligence and strict liability based on possessing a special status. The three status based defenses are (i) charitable immunity; (ii) interfamily immunity; and (iii) sovereign immunity. These three immunity defenses mean that a defendant cannot be sued for negligence or strict liability because of the policy reasons of protecting charities, family members, and sovereign entities from suit.

Charitable Immunity

Entities engaged in charitable or non-profit activities (such as schools, churches, and some hospitals) were traditionally immune from tort suits. This immunity meant that a charitable entity could not be sued for negligence or strict liability. The rationale for the immunity was that threat of law suit might deter people from engaging in such socially beneficial work. The second rationale was to protect the charitable entities from suit by beneficiaries of the charities, who were not happy with the entity's work. The courts wanted simply to stay out of these disputes. Under modern tort law, most states have gotten rid of the charitable immunity on the grounds that charitable entities can engage in conduct that cause harm, and the state wants to deter such activities. The treatment of charitable immunity varies greatly from state to state. No state offers blanket immunity for charitable entities. Some states retain immunity for volunteers who work for charitable entities. You may discuss these issues in greater detail in your course, but at a general level, you should be aware of the immunity and the policy reasons that justified it as well as the reasons for abrogating it.

Intrafamily Immunity

Traditionally, one spouse could not sue another for any tort claim. In the United States, the traditional rule also applied to suits against parents by children. The justification for these immunities rested on the need to protect family harmony, the court's deference to familial relationships, especially parenting decisions, and the concern with frivolous litigation. Most states have abrogated this immunity in various ways. Some states allow suits between spouses when harm to property or intentional torts are at issue. Most states allow suits against parents by children for intentional torts but retain the immunity when the issue involves traditional parenting functions, such as discipline or child-rearing. Some courts are willing to abrogate the parental immunity in negligence cases when the parents have insurance, and the insurance company is the actual defendant in the suit.

Sovereign Immunity

Traditionally, government and governmental actors could not be sued for tort claims. The rationale was to protect the sovereign from suits that would distract from the governmental function. Immunity has been abrogated through statutes at both the federal and the state level. The Federal Tort Claims Act abrogates the immunity of the United States government for negligence claims unless the act being challenged is a discretionary function of the government, which means an act that is part of the policy making function of the governmental entity or the actor. Most states have abrogated immunity for state and municipal government under statutes that follow the exception for discretionary conduct. Most states allow tort claims for intentional tort or negligence unless the conduct falls under the discretionary function of the governmental entity or actor.

■ PROBLEMS ■

1. Plaintiff signed up for a scuba diving trip. She was an experienced diver and had learned about the trip through the Internet.

When she signed up online for the trip, the registration form included a term that stated: "Customer will not hold the Company liable for any ordinary injury that occurs in the course of the underwater vacation." Plaintiff had read the term and checked it off all with the other portions of the contract.

While underwater, Plaintiff experienced some harm to her ears that resulted from her failure to regulate her breathing while descending. While underwater, Plaintiff also ventured away from the group and into a school of manatees. One of the manatees bumped into Plaintiff, causing her breathing tube to become loose. As she was losing pressure, she was rescued by the leader for the group, an agent of the company, that lead her safely to the surface.

As a result of this accident, Plaintiff suffered injury to her eardrums and experienced problems with her breathing. She brought a suit against the Company for negligence in supervising the group underwater and failure to warn her about the manatees. The jurisdiction in which Plaintiff brought the suit: (1) recognizes comparative negligence; (2) had subsumed most of the common law defenses and claims under comparative negligence, except as indicated below; (3) imposes joint and several liability only if the defendant is found more than 50% at fault; (4) does not allow a plaintiff to recover if the plaintiff is found to be 50% at fault or more.

Plaintiff's damages were found to be as follows: $15,000 for the harm to the eardrums; $30,000 for the attack by the manatees and resulting injury.

Analyze the defenses of assumption of risk and comparative negligence that can be raised under these facts. Consider both majority and minority rules.

Suggested Answers

1. In minority jurisdictions, express assumption of risk and primary assumption of risk survive as defenses while secondary assumption of risk is subsumed under comparative negligence. In

most jurisdictions,, express assumption of risk survives as a defense and both primary and secondary assumption risk are subsumed under comparative negligence.

Applying the law of minority jurisdictions to these facts, the defendants can argue that the damage to the eardrums is an "ordinary injury" whose risk Plaintiff assumed by signing the contract. It seems that the injury arose from Plaintiff's failure to regulate the pressure on her eardrums while descending, a standard problem in diving. Assuming that the risk to the eardrum was caused by Plaintiff's failure to regulate, the implication of this argument would be that Plaintiff would be denied all recovery on the $15,000 as damages to her eardrum. Furthermore, under minority law, the defendants may argue that Plaintiff should be denied all recovery because her wandering off and being hit by the manatees constituted primary assumption of risk. Primary assumption of risk applies to situations where the defendant is deemed not to owe a duty to the plaintiff because the nature of the activity is well known and the risks obvious. If primary assumption of risk applies, Plaintiff will not be able to recover anything since assumption of risk is a complete defense. On the other hand, if her wandering off and being hit are treated as secondary assumption of risk, then Plaintiff's recovery of the $30,000 would be reduced by the percentage of Plaintiff's fault (which the jury found here to be 40%).

Applying majority law to these facts, the analysis of express assumption of risk would be the same as above. Furthermore, the majority of jurisdictions subsumes all implied assumption of risk, whether primary or secondary, under comparative negligence. Therefore, in majority jurisdictions, Plaintiff's injuries from wandering off and being hit will be reduced by her percentage of fault, here 40%.

CHECKLIST FOR DEFENSES TO NEGLIGENCE AND STRICT LIABILITY CLAIMS

A. There are two types of defenses to negligence and strict liability claims: defenses based on the conduct of the plaintiff and defenses based on the status of the defendant.

B. Defenses based on the conduct of the plaintiff.

    1. Assumption of risk: a defense based on voluntary and knowing undertaking of a risky activity.

        a. Express assumption of risk: based on contract, specifically an exculpatory clause. Enforcement of the contract term is based on the *Tunkl* factors:

            (i) the defendant is in a business that is thought suitable for public regulation;

            (ii) the defendant is performing a service of great importance to the public, which is often a matter of practical necessity for some members of the public;

            (iii) the defendant holds himself out as willing to perform the service for any member of the public who seeks it;

            (iv) because of the necessity of the service provided, the defendant has a bargaining advantage against members of the public who seek the service;

            (v) the defendant seeks exculpation through a standard adhesion contract and does not provide the option of obtaining protection against injury by paying additional fees;

            (vi) the defendant in rendering service obtains control over the person or property of the person obtaining the service.

    b. Primary assumption of risk: applies to inherent and known risks of an activity when carried out according to the rules of the game;

    c. Secondary, or implied assumption of risk: applies to plaintiff's voluntary and knowing undertaking of an activity outside of an express contract.

2. Contributory negligence: applies to plaintiff's unreasonable conduct that caused plaintiff's injury.

    a. Applies only to negligence claims.

    b. Completely bars recovery by the plaintiff.

    c. Last clear chance doctrine allows the plaintiff to rebut the defense if the plaintiff can show that the defendant had the chance to avoid the accident.

3. Comparative negligence: requires the court to compare the relative fault of the parties and express the relative contribution of the parties to the injuries in percentage terms.

    a. Percentages are used to allocate the damages to the plaintiff. Under a pure system, plaintiff recovers the percentage of damages that are attributed to the defendants. Under a modified system, plaintiff recovers the percentage of damages only if the defendants have a greater percentage than the plaintiff.

    b. Only four states and the District of Columbia retain contributory negligence.

    c. States vary in how assumption of risk is treated under comparative negligence.

        (i) All states retain express assumption of risk as a complete defense.

        (ii) Some states subsume secondary assumption of risk under comparative negligence while retaining primary assumption of risk as a separate defense.

(iii) Other states subsume both primary and secondary assumption of risk under comparative negligence.

C. Defenses based on the status of the defendant.

1. Charitable immunity: all states have abrogated with some retaining immunity from negligence for volunteers in charitable entities.

2. Interfamily immunity: most states have abrogated spousal immunity and some states have abrogated parental immunity.

3. Sovereign immunity: abrogation through statute at the federal and state levels.

CHAPTER 10

Multiple Defendants

GENERAL APPROACH

When multiple defendants are found liable for a tort claim, special issues arise. First, tort law allows recovery against one of many defendants for the entire judgment in favor of a plaintiff. The single defendant subsequently must proceed against the other defendants for their individual contribution. Recovery against one of many defendants is known as joint and several liability, which you should distinguish from joint liability and several liability. Second, tort law allows recovery against a party who is responsible for or in control of the defendants who actually committed the tort. This concept is known as vicarious liability, which applies most often in the area of employment law where the employer is liable for the torts of an employee when they occur in the scope of employment. Third, the issues of joint and several liability and vicarious liability can raise special issues under comparative negligence. This chapter will help you navigate these three issues.

JOINT AND SEVERAL LIABILITY

Under joint and several liability, one of a group of defendants can be held liable for the full judgment won by the plaintiff against the group. The one defendant that is liable for the full judgment must go after the remaining defendants for their share of liability.

Do not confuse joint and several liability with several liability or joint liability. Several liability means that each defendant is liable only for the specific injury caused. Joint liability arises in the case where one of many defendants caused plaintiff's injury but it is not possible to determine which defendant. The concept of joint liability is illustrated by the case of *Summers v. Tice*, discussed in Chapter Five. Under joint liability, the burden shifts to the individual defendants to show that each did not cause the injury. Under joint and several liability, plaintiff can show that a group of defendants caused the injury and can obtain judgment against one defendant in the group.

Joint and several liability arises in one of three situations: (i) concerted action, (ii) joint duty, or (iii) indivisible harm.

If a group of individuals act in concert and their concerted act causes harm to the plaintiff, then joint and several liability applies. A classic example is a group of individuals conspiring to hurt a plaintiff. But the concerted action need not be tortious. For example, if a group of individuals engage in an activity like hunting, drag racing or speed boating, then this concerted action can be the basis for joint and several liability if someone is injured.

If a group of individuals act in a manner that creates a joint duty not to do harm, then joint and several liability applies. An example of joint duty is the relationship between a manufacturer, a distributor, and a retailer of a product. If the product harms someone because it is defective, then the manufacturer, distributor, and retailer owe a joint duty to the injured party. The victim can go after any one of these three for a tort claim under joint and several liability. Another example of a joint duty is a harm that arises from a business partnership that, for example, sells a defective product or negligently performs a service. A plaintiff can go after one of the partners for a tort claim under joint and several liability.

Finally, if individuals are acting independently but their acts result in an indivisible harm to a person, then joint and several liability applies. Suppose someone is driving behind someone who is travelling too slowly and in front of someone who is travelling too fast. Because of the poor driving of both the person in front and behind, there is an accident resulting in the driver in the middle being injured and suffering damage to the car. There is no feasible way to separate the harm caused by the slow driving from the harm caused by the fast driving. This case is one of indivisible harm, and the accident victim can bring a tort claim against either driver under joint and several liability.

Joint and several liability is not a tort claim. You should understand it as a legal device for bringing suit against one party for injuries caused by a group of individuals. Keep in mind these three instances where joint and several liability arise. Also keep in mind that in each of these instances, plaintiff still has to establish a tort claim, whether an intentional tort, negligence, or strict liability.

If a defendant is found liable under joint and several liability, the defendant is liable for the entire judgment, but can bring an action against the other defendants to recover their share of liability. Traditionally, this claim was brought as a claim for indemnity. Under the indemnity claim, the defendant held liable would seek indemnification from the other defendants. Under modern tort law, the claim is for contribution. The defendant held liable would bring a separate suit to recover the other defendants' contributions to the injury. Under comparative negligence, each of these other defendants would have been found liable for a percentage of their fault. These percentages would apply in a contribution action to apportion liability among the defendants.

As part of recent tort form, most states have modified their rules for joint and several liability. Some states have gotten rid of joint and several liability altogether. Others have limited joint and several liability in different ways. For example, some states do not allow joint and several liability if the plaintiff has been found to be negligent. As another example of tort reform, some states allow joint and several liability only against a defendant whose percentage fault falls above a particular numerical threshold, usually 50 per cent. Your professor may delve into the particular modifications of joint and several liability that is applicable to the jurisdiction where you are studying. Understand, however, that the policies for reforming joint and several liability tend to be fairly common across states. The first policy is curing the apparent unfairness in holding one defendant for the full amount of liability. The second policy in favor of reform is the incentive joint and several liability gives for litigation promotion, especially suits against deep pockets. On the other side, joint and several liability is defended as an effective means for a plaintiff to recover when some defendants are insolvent or outside the jurisdiction of a favorable venue. In analyzing a joint and several liability issue, make sure you can recognize (i) when and how the doctrine applies, (ii) the particular reforms to joint and several liability that your professor might emphasize, and (iii) the policies for and against joint and several liability.

VICARIOUS LIABILITY

Under vicarious liability, a defendant is held liable for the torts committed by someone over whom they have control or for whom they have responsibility. Unlike with joint and several liability, the defendant can be held liable for doing nothing at all. Vicarious liability arises in four situations: (i) the vicarious liability of an employer for the torts committed by an employee in the scope of employment, (ii) the vicarious liability of a hiring party for the torts committed by an independent contractor who is engaged in an act for which duties are non-delegable, (iii) in some jurisdictions, the vicarious liability of a parent for the intentional or malicious act of a child, and (iv) in some jurisdictions, the vicarious liability of the owner of an automobile for the torts committed by a permitted driver of the vehicle. Keep in mind that as in all tort cases, the plaintiff can recover only once for an injury suffered. So the plaintiff can recover either against the actual person who engaged in the tortious conduct or against the person who has vicarious liability.

Before we discuss each of these cases of vicarious liability, let us make clear some important distinctions. First, make sure you understand the distinction between vicarious liability and joint and several liability. Under joint and several liability, each defendant has acted in a way that is tortious; the law makes it easier for a plaintiff to sue one of the defendants for the entire judgment.

Under vicarious liability, a defendant is found liable for not doing anything tortious but for being in a relationship involving responsibility or control over the person who actually committed a tort. You can think about vicarious liability as a derivative liability: a defendant is held liable if the person over whom he has responsibility or control committed a tort. Even though the concepts are different, they can work in tandem. For example, in a partnership, one partner is vicariously liable for the torts committed by another partner. But a partnership can also give rise to joint and several liability. So, if Stan and Bob are in a partnership, and Bob commits a tort in the scope of the partnership, then Stan will be vicariously liable for Bob's tort and can be sued under joint and several liability for the full amount of a plaintiff's injuries. Once found liable under joint and several liability, Stan can then sue Bob in a contribution action for Bob's share of the liability.

Second, distinguish joint and several liability from a claim for negligent supervision or entrustment. In many instances, the party who has responsibility or control over the party committing a tort can be found independently liable for negligence in unreasonably supervising or unreasonably entrusting the person who injured the plaintiff. For example, an employer hires an employee to deliver pizzas. In the course of delivering pizzas, the employee negligently or intentionally runs into someone with the car. The employer is vicariously liable for the employee's torts. In addition, the plaintiff has a potential claim against the employer for negligence in not properly supervising the employee or in entrusting the employee with an automobile. As a matter of litigation strategy, there is a good reason why a plaintiff would want to raise both the vicarious liability and the negligent supervision or entrustment claims. Vicarious liability is a derivative claim; the employer's liability derives from the employee's. If the employee is found not to be liable, then the employer cannot be vicariously liable. But the employer might still be liable for negligence in entrusting or supervising the employee.

Here are some specific issues to remember about vicarious liability in the four situations in which it arises.

Employer vicariously liable for employee: The big issue here is whether the employee's tortious act occurred in the scope of employment. This issue is particularly important when an intentional tort is involved. Suppose an employee, while delivering a product for the employer, sees an enemy and beats him up. The employee has committed a battery, but the employer is arguably not vicariously liable because the battery was committed outside the scope of employment. The employee, on these facts, seems to be carrying out his own vendetta against an enemy. Now suppose that the employee is a bouncer at a bar and uses great physical force to remove a customer from the bar. In this case, if the bouncer has committed a battery against the customer, then the employer can be vicariously liable because the act was in the scope of employment.

Independent contractor engaged in activity involving a non-delegable duty: An independent contractor, as distinguished from an employee, is hired to perform some discrete and well-defined projects. In general, a hiring party is not vicariously liable for the torts committed by an independent contractor committed in the course of carrying out the contract. However, if the independent contractor is engaged in a hazardous activity, then the hiring party cannot escape liability by having the independent contractor engage in the activity. For example, suppose a company hires someone to engage in explosive blasting to bring down a building. Blasting is considered a hazardous activity. The hiring party will be vicariously liable for the torts of the blasting company because the hiring party is not allowed under the law to delegate the duty to engage in hazardous activity safely to someone else.

Parent vicarious liability for children: Traditionally, parents were not vicariously liable for the torts of their children. Many jurisdictions, however, have made parents vicariously liable for the intentional torts committed by children. Some jurisdictions impose vicarious liability only if the harmful proclivities of children are known to the parent.

Owner of automobile vicariously liable for driver: Some jurisdictions impose vicarious liability on the owner of an automobile for the tortious acts of a known drivers. Some jurisdictions require the owner to be in the car at the time of the tortious act; other jurisdictions do not. Some jurisdictions have a family purpose doctrine that imposes vicarious liability on the owner of an auto-mobile for torts committed by another family member driving the car under the theory that the automobile serves a family purpose. Outside the automobile context, there is no vicarious liability for simply providing someone with an instrument that can be used to commit a tort. Liability for providing someone the instrumentality to commit a tort is based on a negligent entrustment or supervision theory.

SPECIAL ISSUES UNDER COMPARATIVE NEGLIGENCE

Multiple defendants pose important issues for comparative negligence regimes. These issues have prompted moves for tort reform in many states, and we have mentioned some of these reforms above in he section on joint and several liability. In this section, we will emphasize three issues: (i) the treatment of settle-ments, (ii) the doctrine of imputed contributory negligence, and (iii) the issue of intentional tort and negligence claims.

Settlements: Traditionally, a settlement reached with one defendant would dismiss the claims against all defendants. The modern approach is to allow partial settlements whereby a plaintiff can settle with one or more of the defendants and continue the suit to judgment against the remaining ones. A settlement raises two sets of legal issues. The first has to do with offsets of the settlement against the final judgment. The second has to do with contribution actions against and by settling defendants.

All states will offset settlements against the final judgment for the plaintiff. States differ, however, in how the settlement amount is used to offset the judgment. Some states will offset the final judgment dollar for dollar from the settlement amount. Other states will offset the final judgment by the proportionate share of the settling defendant's comparative liability. In *McDermott, Inc. v. AmCLYDE*, 511 U.S. 202 (1994), the United States Supreme Court adopted the proportionate share approach as the appropriate means of offset in a tort suit brought under admiralty jurisdiction. The Court reasoned that the dollar-for-dollar amount tended to push a suit to early settlement for an amount lower than what would be obtained at judgment. The problem, however, with the proportionate share approach is difficulty of administration, especially if not all the defendants have been joined into the suit. Pay attention to what your professor says about the treatment of settlements in the jurisdiction where you are studying tort law, and as always be alert to the policy debate between the choice of the dollar-per-dollar approach and the proportionate share approach.

As far as the contribution issue, all states do not allow contribution against a settling defendant, whose liability has been exhausted by the settlement. However, the general trend is to allow the settling defendant to obtain contribution from non-settling defendants if the settlement amount is greater than the settling defendant's proportionate share of liability and if the settling defendant has obtained a release from the other defendants.

Imputed contributory negligence: In comparative negligence cases, the negligence of a third party can sometimes be imputed to the plaintiff. For example, the negligence of an employer sometimes can be imputed to an employee who is a plaintiff in a law suit. The effect of imputed contributory negligence is to reduce the recovery of a plaintiff even if the plaintiff was not at fault. Because of the unfairness created by the rule, many jurisdictions have done away with the rule. But some jurisdictions maintain a version of the imputed contributory negligence doctrine. Specifically, some jurisdictions do not impute contributory negligence if negligence is not imputed through vicarious liability. The effect of this version of imputed contributory negligence is not impute contributory negligence in most situations, such as the parent-child context, or in most situations involving personal property. Under this rule, it is left open whether contributory negligence will be imputed in cases where negligence clearly would be imputed, such as the employer-employee context. Some jurisdictions used to adopt the "both ways rule," under which contributory negligence would be imputed if negligence was imputed. Almost all jurisdictions have done away with the "both ways rule" because of the harshness for plaintiffs. Consequently, imputed contributory negligence seems to be a less important doctrine, but one that your professor may talk about in class because of the policy concerns and the application of vicarious liability.

Mixture of intentional torts and negligence: Jurisdictions struggle over what to do if a plaintiff brings intentional tort claims against some defendants and negligence claims against others. From a comparative negligence perspective, it does not seem to make sense to compare the negligence of one defendant with the intentional conduct of another. On the other hand, if the comparative negligence regime is a means of apportioning damages based on fault, it should not make a difference whether fault is based on intent or negligence, or even strict liability. Some jurisdictions have adopted a comparative fault perspective, treating the apportionment issue as one of allocating damages among defendants based on their comparative contribution to causing the plaintiff's injury. Other jurisdictions have adopted statutory approaches under which all the torts are combined for proportionate fault purposes, but intent and other factors are taken into consideration for the purposes of joint and several liability or enhancements to damages. Be aware of this issue and pay attention to what your professor says about how your jurisdiction handles this issue.

■ PROBLEMS ■

1. Plaintiff signed up for a scuba diving trip. She was an experienced diver and had learned about the trip through the Internet. When she signed up online for the trip, the registration form included a term that stated: "Customer will not hold the Company liable for any ordinary injury that occurs in the course of the underwater vacation." Plaintiff had read the term and checked it off all with the other portions of the contract.

While underwater, Plaintiff experienced some harm to her ears that resulted from her failure to regulate her breathing while descending. While underwater, Plaintiff also ventured away from the group and into a school of manatees. One of the manatees bumped into Plaintiff, causing her breathing tube to become loose. As she was losing pressure, she was rescued by the leader for the group, an agent of the company, that lead her safely to the surface.

As a result of this accident, Plaintiff suffered injury to her eardrums and experienced problems with her breathing. She brought a suit against the Company for negligence in supervising the group underwater and failure to warn her about the manatees. The jurisdiction in which Plaintiff brought the suit: (1) recognizes comparative negligence; (2) had subsumed most of the common law defenses and claims under comparative negligence, except as indicated below; (3) imposes joint and several liability only if the defendant is found more than 50% at fault; (4) does not allow a plaintiff to recover if the plaintiff is found to be 50% at fault or more.

Plaintiff's damages were found to be as follows: $15,000 for the harm to the eardrums; $30,000 for the attack by the manatees and resulting injury.

Answer each of the following questions, using this information for each question.

(A) The leader of the group, like other agents of the Company, is an independent contractor. As a condition of agency, the leader signed a contract agreeing to indemnify the Company for any claims brought against the Company resulting from accidents that occurred during a trip. Explain what an indemnity is and the possible effects on the litigation between Plaintiff and Company.

(B) Suppose the leader is joined as a defendant in the litigation between Plaintiff and Company. The jury determines that Plaintiff was 40% at fault and the the Company and leader were each 30% at fault. Explain whether Plaintiff can recover and use joint and several liability under these facts.

(C) The jurisdiction requires the judgment to be reduced by the percentage of fault of a settling party. Explain the implications of this rule for the facts in (B) if the leader settles with Plaintiff.

Suggested Answers

1.   (A) An indemnity is an agreement between two individuals A and B under which A becomes liable to B under certain conditions if B is found liable to a third party. In this case, since the leader agreed to indemnify the Company for claims brought against the Company resulting from accidents that occurred during a trip, the Company can seek indemnity from the leader if the Company is found liable to Plaintiff. Most likely, the Company will seek to join the leader into the law suit as a co-defendant.

(B) In this jurisdiction, a plaintiff is denied recovery if he is found to be 50% or more at fault. Here, Plaintiff's fault falls below 50% and so she can recover. She will be able to recover 60% of her judgment from the defendants. In this jurisdiction, joint and several liability applies only for a defendant who is more than 50% at fault. Here neither defendant meets that threshold. As a result, joint and several liability will not available to the plaintiff. The Company and the leader will be independently liable for their respective shares of the judgment, in other words, 30% of the $45,000 each.

(C) In this jurisdiction, plaintiff's judgment is reduced by the share of fault attributable to a settling defendant. Here, Plaintiff can recover 30% of the judgment from Company and must bear any shortfall between the amount of the settlement and the amount of the judgment attributable to the leader based on fault. On the other hand, Plaintiff will retain any excess in the settlement above the share of the judgment.

CHECKLIST FOR MULTIPLE DEFENDANTS

A. Joint and several liability: allows a plaintiff to obtain the judgment for the full amount of damages against one of many defendants.

   1. It should be distinguished from joint liability and several liability.

2. It arises in one of three situations:

     a. Concerted action.

     b. Joint duty.

     c. Indivisible harm.

3. The defendant found liable under joint and several liability can obtain a judgment against the other defendants for the proportionate share under a claim for indemnity or for contribution.

B. Vicarious liability: imputes liability to a party based on the tortious conduct of someone over whom the party has responsibility or control.

1. Under vicarious liability, a party can be liable even though they did not commit a tort.

2. The party can also be held liable under joint and several liability.

3. The party can also be held liable under a negligent supervision or a negligent entrustment claim.

4. Vicarious liability arises in four situations:

     a. Liability of an employer for the torts committed by an employee in the scope of employment.

     b. Liability of a hiring party for the activity of an independent contractor involving a nondelegable duty.

     c. In some jurisdictions, liability of a parent for the intentional or malicious acts of a child.

     d. In some jurisdictions, liability of the owner of an automobile for the tortious acts of a driver.

C. Special Issues Under Comparative Negligence.

1. A plaintiff can settle with one defendant and continue litigation with the remaining defendants.

     a. The amount of settlement will be offset against the final judgment either on a dollar-per-dollar amount or on the proportionate share of the settling defendant's liability.

b. Non-settling defendants cannot seek contribution from a settling defendant.

c. A settling defendant can seek contribution from non-settling defendants if the amount of settlement is greater than the proportionate share of liability and the settling defendant received a release from the non-settling ones.

2. Imputed contributory negligence imputes the negligence of a third party to the plaintiff. Jurisdictions that adopt the doctrine impute contributory negligence only if negligence is imputed.

3. Many jurisdictions grapple with the issue of how to handle claims of intentional torts against some defendants and negligence against others. Some jurisdictions treat all tort claims under a proportionate fault approach. Others have adopted statutes to treat intentional tort claims differently for the purposes of apportionment.

CHAPTER 11

Products Liability

GENERAL APPROACH

Products liability is a topic covered in most first year Torts courses. The subject allows your professor to integrate the various topics you have covered throughout the course and provides a basis to discuss the policies of product safety, compensation, and deterrence. There are several distinct legal claims that fall under products liability: negligence, strict liability, and misrepresentation. Be careful in understanding and applying each of these three claims. You should understand that each claim provides a way for a plaintiff to obtain recovery against a defendant for manufacturing, distributing, and selling a defective product that injured the plaintiff. Keep in mind, however, the basic principle that the plaintiff can obtain only one recovery for an injury. So even if the plaintiff is successful on all three claims, the plaintiff can recover only once for a particular injury. The three separate claims provide different legal bases for the plaintiff to seek legal redress from the defendant.

This chapter goes through negligence, strict liability, and misrepresentation separately, explaining the legal basis and origin for each claim and contrasting them. The chapter ends with a discussion of special defenses that arise in products liability claims. The section of special defenses introduces one new concept and also presents a review of the topics from previous chapters.

NEGLIGENCE

The plaintiff has to establish duty, breach, causation, and damages, just as we discussed in Chapters Three through Six. In the context of a products liability claim, a plaintiff must establish that the defendant owed a duty not to manufacture, sell, or distribute a dangerous product, that the defendant breached this duty through unreasonable conduct, that the unreasonable conduct was the factual and legal cause of the plaintiff's injuries, and that the plaintiff suffered damages.

One issue you will concentrate on is that of duty. In English common law, lack of privity of contract meant that there was no duty owed in tort law. This meant that if someone bought a dangerous product from a seller, and the dangerous product injured the purchaser, then the purchaser could not sue the manufacturer because the contract was with the seller. Another example of the privity rule is provided by injury to an employee. If an employee was injured by a dangerous product on the job, then the employee could not sue the manufacturer or the seller of the product because there was no privity of contract between the employee and the manufacturer or the seller. Yet another example of privity is provided by injury to third parties. Suppose someone bought an automobile that was defective in some way. A passenger in the car is injured by the defect. Under the privity rule, the passenger could not sue the manufacturer or the seller since there was no privity of contract.

The logic of the privity rule is that each party in the chain of contract would have a claim against the other. So in the first example of the purchaser injured by a dangerous product, the purchaser would have to sue the seller for the dangerous product and the seller would in turn have a claim against the distributor, who in turn would have a claim against the manufacturer, and so on. The argument is that this provided a more efficient way of managing the risk and a more effective way for courts to manage the disputes. The practice, however, did not follow the theory, and the privity rule became a way for companies to avoid liability.

The privity rule was done away with for products liability in *MacPherson v. Buick Motor Co.*, 111 N.E. 1050 (1916), a famous Judge Cardozo opinion that set the ball rolling for modern products liability law. The key passage from the opinion is:

> if the nature of a thing is such that it is reasonably certain to place life and limb in peril *when negligently made*, it is then a thing of danger. Its nature gives warning of the consequences to be expected. If to the element of danger there is added knowledge that the thing *will be used other than the purchaser, and used without new tests,* then, *irrespective of contract*, the manufacture of this thing of danger is under a *duty to make it carefully.* [emphases added] *Id.*

There are two points to understand from this passage. The first is the language "irrespective of contract." This statement means that privity of contract is irrelevant when a manufacturer of a product is concerned. Subsequent cases extended Judge Cardozo's point to include distributors and retailers. The second is the nature of the duty created by the court. It is a duty to make a product carefully so that the product will not injure someone. The court reasons that a product negligently made is one that is dangerous to life and limb. Therefore, there is a duty to prevent harm to others by not negligently making a product.

The *MacPherson* decision created a duty not to make a product negligently. Subsequent cases extended this duty to distributors and retailers of products. Subsequent cases also addressed the issue of what it means to make a product negligently. This issue gets to the element of breach. All of the methods of showing breach discussed in Chapter Four apply here. A plaintiff has to show that a manufacturer acted unreasonably in making or designing a product. A plaintiff can introduce evidence, for example, that the manufacturer fell below the industry standard in making or designing the product, or that under a BpL analysis, the manufacturer failed to adequately make or design the product. In other words, the plaintiff shows that the duty to use reasonable care in making a product was breached by the defendant using any of the standard arguments we discussed in Chapter Four. Finally, the usual arguments for causation and damages discussed in Chapters Five and Six apply in order for the plaintiff to complete the claim for negligence.

STRICT LIABILITY

A strict products liability claim has four elements: (i) the duty not to manufacture, distribute, or sell a defective product; (ii) breach of the duty by manufacturing, distributing, or selling a defective product; (iii) causation of the injury; and (iv) damages. The main difference between a negligence and a strict liability claim for a defective product is that a plaintiff does not have to show unreasonable conduct on the part of the defendant to make a successful strict products liability claim. For a strict products liability claim, a plaintiff has to show that the defendant sold a defective product and that the product caused plaintiff's injuries. The big issue under a strict products liability the claim is showing that the product was defective.

To understand what it means for a product to be a defective, it is useful to understand a brief genesis of the strict products liability claim. In most jurisdictions, the strict products liability claim developed from the contract claims for breach of express or implied warranties. Under contract law, the purchaser of a product, and in some instances users of the product, had a claim for breach of an express or implied warranty that was part of the contract for sale of the product. Breach of the warranties would be shown by the failure of the product to meet the consumer's expectations of the how the product was supposed to function. Strict products liability arose from the breach of warranty claims that imposed liability on the seller of a product regardless of fault. Some courts expanded the contract claims to be brought as tort claims with the resulting damages available under tort law (see Chapter Seven). Other courts analogized the sale of a defective product to the escape principle or an ultrahazardous activity, either of which could provide the basis for a strict liability claim (see Chapter Eight).

Section 402A of the Second Restatement of Torts famously summarizes the principles of strict product liability. You will most likely read the provision in your Torts class. This section imposes liability *without regard to fault or intent and without regard to privity of contract* on

   (1) someone *engaged in the business of selling* a product,

   (2) when the product is sold in a defective condition *unreasonably dangerous to the consumer, user, or his property,*

   (3) for the *physical harm* to the user or consumer or his *property,*

   (4) if the product is expected to and does reach the user or consumer *without substantial change in the condition* in which it is sold.

Let us discuss the emphasized portions in more detail. The "without regard to fault or intent" means that the liability is strict. The "without regard to privity of contract" means that lack of a contractual relationship does not preclude tort liability. The "engaged in the business of selling" means that liability attaches to anyone who sells the product to someone else, covering the manufacturer, distributor, and the retailer of a product. Pay attention to the word "engaged in the business," which means that occasional sellers of products are not strictly liable for selling a defective product. They, however, could be liable under negligence if a plaintiff can show unreasonable conduct. The language "unreasonably dangerous to the consumer, user, or his property" is the basis for what makes a product defective, as discussed in greater detail below. The language "physical harm" and "property" covers the kind of damages that can be recovered; review the materials in Chapters Six and Seven in greater detail on this point. Finally, "without substantial change in the condition" covers a common defense in strict product liability cases: alterations made by the purchaser or user that are the cause of the injury to the plaintiff.

What is a defect?

The key issue in a strict products liability case is what makes a product defective. Under the language of Section 402A, a product is defective if it is "unreasonably dangerous." The use of the word "unreasonable" seems to introduce negligence into a strict liability claim and has resulted in lots of confusion. To keep the issue clear, note that "unreasonably dangerous" here applies to the product, and not to the conduct of the defendant. The question is not whether the defendant acted unreasonably, but whether a reasonable person would find the product dangerous. There are some products which have inherent characteristics that are dangerous. Examples are the ability of alcohol to cause intoxication, tobacco to cause disease, or fatty foods to cause obesity. These inherent characteristics are not defects.

There are two types of defects that can provide the basis for a strict product liability claim: (i) a manufacturing defect, (ii) a design defect, or (iii) a warning defect. A plaintiff has to show that one or more of these types of defect existed in order to show that a product was defective.

Manufacturing defect: This type of defect arises in the way a product was put together by the maker of the product. It refers to some flaw in the way the product was put together in the factory where the product was made. In general, a plaintiff does not have to show what that flaw in the factory was. Instead, a plaintiff can simply point to the fact that the product did not work as it was supposed to work in order to establish that the product had a manufacturing defect. For example, if a toaster explodes, or a car catches fire spontaneously, or a tire pops unexpectedly, each of these is an instance of a product not functioning as expected which can be the basis for showing a manufacturing defect. The defendant in these cases, however, may point to other reasons for the unexpected operation, such as wear and tear, alterations, or mishandling by the user, which might explain the unexpected operation of the product. Often, manufacturing defect cases will involve the use of experts to show how the product failed and explain how the product was supposed to operate.

Design defect: This type of defect points to the way in which a product is designed as the explanation for why the product caused injury. For example, the failure to use safety glass on an automobile or the failure to include a safety device on a lawnmower may constitute a design defect. Most jurisdictions require a plaintiff to show a reasonable alternative design as a requirement to prove a design defect. To meet the requirement of a reasonable alternative design, a plaintiff has to show that it was feasible to design the product in an alternative way that would have avoided or mitigated the damages.

There are two standards to determine when the design of a product is defective. The first is the consumer expectation test, which looks to a reasonable consumer's perceptions of a product to determine whether a product is defectively designed. The problem with this test is often products are technically complex. Consequently, a reasonable consumer may not have any basis to determine whether a product is defectively designed. As a result, courts have introduced a second test for design defect, called the risk-utility test to determine whether a design is defective. Under the risk-utility test, a plaintiff must show that the risks of a particular design outweigh its utility to establish that a design is defective. The following factors are often relevant to the risk-utility analysis: (i) usefulness and desirability of the product; (ii) likelihood and serious of injury a product could cause, (iii) availability of a safer substitute product; (iv) manufacturer's ability to eliminate the unsafe features without impairing the usefulness or aggravating the risks; (v) user's ability to avoid danger by the exercise of care; (vi) user's anticipated awareness of the dangers based on the obvious condition, warnings, or general public knowledge; and (vii) feasibility of loss spreading by the manufacturer through setting the price or carrying insurance.

Warning defects: A seller has a duty to impose warnings about dangers of a product that the seller knows about or should know about. These warnings should be obvious and reasonable to the user in order to be adequate. There is no duty to warn about obvious or generally known dangers.

MISREPRESENTATION

Your professor may discuss a claim of misrepresentation claim as part of products liability in your Torts class. It is common to include a misrepresentation claim as part of a products liability suit. The idea is that the seller of the product misled consumers about the features of the product and this misleading statement made the consumer buy and use a harmful product that he would not have purchased but for the misrepresentation. We present the elements of misrepresentation in Chapter Thirteen under Business Torts. We mention it here because misrepresentation claims are increasingly common in products liability cases in conjunction with claims that the seller failed to adequately warn about the product.

SPECIAL DEFENSES IN PRODUCTS LIABILITY CLAIMS

The defenses discussed in Chapter Nine apply in products liability claims based on negligence and on strict liability. Here, we emphasize four special defenses that arise in products liability cases: (i) not a product; (ii) state of the art; (iii) conduct of the plaintiff; and (iv) preemption.

Not a product: Strict products liability claims apply only to products and not to services or to sale of land. In the context of real estate, strict products liability cases have been applied to the sale of structures, specifically specially designed or modified homes. In the context of services, strict products liability has been applied to the products that may be part of the provision of a service. For example, the provision of a beauty service, such as a haircut, would not be the basis for strict products liability, but the use of beauty care products, like a shampoo, would be. Courts have also made distinctions between products and services in other areas. For example, electricity transmission through power lines is a service, but once it enters a home through a meter, it is deemed a product. Furthermore, charts and maps are considered products, but books and games are considered information services and therefore cannot be the basis for strict products liability. Finally, your professor may address the special case of software, which one jurisdiction has found to be a product for the purposes of strict product liability. Keep in mind that even though strict products liability does not apply to a case involving services, negligence does.

State of the art: This defense arises in the context of claims for strict product liability for a design defect. Under this defense, a defendant claims not to be liable because a product's design met the standard for the product at the time the product was made. In other words, the product met the state of the art and therefore cannot be the basis for liability. Some courts reject this defense on the grounds that product designs need to be updated to meet improved and increased knowledge about technology and product design.

Conduct of the plaintiff: The plaintiff's operation and maintenance of a product can be a defense to negligence and strict products liability claims. The defense is one of contributory or comparative negligence. Your professor may raise the issue of comparative negligence as a defense in a strict products liability case because of the tension between comparative negligence and strict liability. Keep in mind, as discussed in Chapter Nine, that comparative negligence can be used as a defense in strict products liability cases. The tension between comparative negligence and strict liability is less important as many jurisdictions move to comparative fault perspective for the purposes of apportionment as we discussed in Chapter Ten.

Preemption: This defense arises whenever a federal safety standard, such as one under the Consumer Product Safety Commission, Food & Drug Administration, or other federal agency, is at issue. Under the defense of preemption, a plaintiff cannot pursue a state tort claim because it conflicts with federal law and creates a contrary safety standard.

There are two types of preemption: express and implied. Express preemption arises when a federal statute or regulation expressly states that no state claims are permitted under the law. This type of preemption is rare because state tort law is viewed as complementary to federal safety regulation in most cases. Implied preemption is more common and has been the subject of the most of the cases your professor might present on this topic. Implied preemption arises from a potential conflict between a federal standard and a standard under state law. For example, a federal requirement that a cigarette manufacturer had to place a warning on cigarette packets was found to pre-empt a failure to warn claim, but not an express warranty claim under contract law. See *Cipollone v. Liggett Group*, 505 U.S. 504 (1992). In addition, a federal requirement that air bags were optional during a particular time period was held to preempt a design defect claim for harms caused by a car that did not have an air bag during the period when they were optional. See *Geier v. American Honda Motor Co.*, 529 U.S. 861 (2000). When a state claim imposes a standard that conflicts with a federal standard, the federal standard trumps.

Preemption can be a very complicated analysis because it requires a careful attention to federal statutes and to state tort law. Break down the preemption analysis into the following steps. First, see if the federal statute or regulation expressly states that no state tort claim can be brought. If there is express language, then there is express preemption. Second, see if the federal statute or regulation defines a safety standard. If it does, then ask whether the state tort claim imposes a standard that conflicts with the federal standard. If the state claim does, then the federal standard trumps, and the plaintiff cannot bring the state claim.

Also, make sure you understand the difference between the defense of preemption and the use of statutes to establish negligence per se in a negligence claim. Here are the principal differences. First, preemption applies to all tort claims, whether brought under negligence, strict liability, or intentional torts. The use of statutes for negligence per se applies only in a negligence claim. Second, preemption is a defense that dismisses a plaintiff's claim. The use of a statute establishes breach as a matter of law in a negligence claim and therefore is part of a plaintiff's case. In some jurisdictions, the use of a statute is evidence of breach and therefore serves as evidence in a negligence case. Preemption, however, is a defense in every jurisdiction.

In addition, distinguish preemption from the defense of compliance with a regulatory statute. Compliance with a statute might be a factor in considering the reasonableness of the defendant's conduct or the reasonableness of a product design. In general, compliance with a statute is not dispositive. If the statute at issue preempts the tort claim, either expressly or implicitly, then the state tort claim is dismissed because federal law trumps all state law.

RESTATEMENT (THIRD) OF TORTS: PRODUCTS LIABILITY

The Restatement (Third) summarizes juridical developments in tort law from the 1980s and 1990s. We will discuss some of those changes here. They should be understood in conjunction with the discussion of the law above. Since this area of law is changing, please consult with your instructor about particular rules that would apply to your jurisdiction and to your particular course.

The major change is the division of the law of products liability by type of defect as opposed to whether the claim is based on negligence or strict liability. Courts recognized these types of defect before the adoption of the Restatement (Third). But the Restatement (Third) uses the three types of defects to organize the law. Although the concepts of negligence and strict liability are still relevant, the Restatement (Third) starts from categorizing the type of defect at issue: manufacturing, design, or inadequate warning or instructions.

Liability for a manufacturing defect under the Restatement (Third) is strict. A manufacturing defect exists if the product differs from its intended design even if all possible care was taken to manufacture the product. Circumstantial evidence such as the accident itself can be used to show the existence of a manufacturing defect.

Liability for a design defect under the Restatement (Third) is based on the risk-utility test. The Restatement (Third) does away with the consumer expectations test as a separate test for the existence of a design defect. However, consumer expectations may be a factor in considering the risk or utility of the product design.

In addition, the plaintiff has the burden to show a reasonable alternative design whose absence makes the product not reasonably safe. The comments do allow a plaintiff to show that a design is "manifestly unreasonable." An example would be a toy gun that shoots hard pellets that might harm someone. Liability would attach to a manifestly unreasonable design even if there is no safer alternative design.

Liability for inadequate warnings or instructions attaches if the foreseeable risk of harm posed by the product could have been avoided or reduced with reasonable warnings or instructions. Reasonableness is based on the circumstances and is based on such factors as "content and comprehensibility, intensity of expression, and the characteristics of the expected used group."

■ PROBLEMS ■

1. Defendant sells cigarette lighters in the shape of dragons. The lighters were made as part of product tie-in with an R-rated movie called "Dragon Wars." Defendant made the lighters under a license from Motion Picture Studio that made "Dragon Wars." Plaintiff, a ten year old, found one of these lighters thrown away by the side of the road. Plaintiff playing with the lighter produced a flame. The flame made the lighter become hot, and Plaintiff dropped lighter on himself. As a result, his clothes caught fire and he suffered severe burns.

A. Analyze Plaintiff's claim against Defendant for negligence.

B. Analyze Plaintiff claim against Defendant for strict product liability.

C. Suppose that the Consumer Product Safety Commission passed a regulation dealing with product tie-ins a few years before Defendant started manufacturing the lighters. The regulation stated that a manufacturer must ensure that product tie-ins aimed at the adult market must be safe for children. The regulation states that safety is to be determined by a reasonableness standard. Analyze whether this regulation would preempt any of the claims discussed in questions A and B above.

Suggested Answers

1.   A. Plaintiff's claim for negligence would rest on showing that Defendant owed a duty to Plaintiff, that the duty was breached by an unreasonable act or omission, that the breach caused Plaintiff's injuries, and that the injuries were legally compensable damages. As for the duty elements, Plaintiff can argue that Defendant could have reasonably foreseen that its product would come into the hands of a child. As for the damage element, Plaintiff has suffered physical injury that would be legally compensable. The difficult part of the case is showing breach and causation. As for breach, Plaintiff would have to point to a specific act or failure to act that was unreasonable. Here, plaintiff would have to point to some act by the defendant, such as a decision how the product was put together or marketed, that fell below the standard of care, as established through custom, knowledge, the BpL analysis, or statute. In addition, Plaintiff could create an inference of unreasonableness via *res ipsa loquitur*. Based on the facts given, Plaintiff might have a difficult time. The strongest fact here is arguably the decision to market a lighter as something that could have been mistaken for a toy without adequate protections against the type of accident that occurred here. The statute mentioned in Part D, below, might be a basis for negligence per se, but the statute seems to establish a reasonableness standard and so is not helpful in articulating a standard of what constitutes unreasonableness. Custom might be some evidence of unreasonableness here as an indication of either how other hazardous tie-ins are marketed or how lighters are marketed. Knowledge of similar sorts of accidents might also be evidence of unreasonableness in making and marketing the product as Defendant did here. Finally, Plaintiff could argue under a BpL analysis that the Defendant's decision to package a lighter as a toy was unreasonable given the costs of choosing an alternative design (B) as compared with the probable injury (pL). Defendant, however, would have equally strong arguments about the reasonableness of marketing a product tied into a

movie aimed at an adult audience.

If Plaintiff can identify an unreasonable act, there is still a causation issue here. Defendant may argue that the abandonment of the lighter and the child's use were acts that would cut off its liability as a superseding cause. However, if Plaintiff can show what the unreasonable act or omission was, Plaintiff would have an argument that the the acts of abandonment and use by a child were foreseeable acts that would justify imposing liability on Defendant. Note that the act of the child may serve as a defense either as contributory negligence or comparative negligence (depending on the jurisdiction). The child's negligence will be determined based on the standard of a child of similar age, experience and maturity although Defendant might argue that the adult standard should apply because playing with a lighter is an adult activity. Finally, assumption of risk is unlikely here as a defense because the plaintiff arguably was not aware of the risks associated with using this particular product.

B.   The strict liability claim would require Plaintiff showing the presence of a defect, either manufacturing, design, or warning, that caused the injury. The presence of a manufacturing defect would require showing that this particular product was put to-gether in a way that created a defective condition unreasonably dangerous. This can be shown through expert testimony or through eyewitness testimony about how this product functioned or was put together. Here, the fact that the lighter became hot may serve as a basis on which to show that the product was manufac-tured defectively. As a practical matter, proof of a manufacturing defect would require examining the product itself. A design defect is established either through the use of a consumer expectations test (for simple designs) or through a risk-utility analysis (for more technical designs). Here, Plaintiff could argue for a consumer expectations test either because the product is a toy or because it is a lighter. Defendant might argue that the product is more technical in its design and support the use of the risk-utility analysis. Here, Plaintiff could argue that the Defendant could have designed the lighter so it would not be mistaken for a toy by a child. Perhaps Defendant could have simply placed a picture of a dragon on the lighter rather than making the entire product look like a dragon. Defendant might argue that the utility of the lighter arose from the novelty of its dragon design. Finally, under the warning defect theory, Plaintiff would need to show that Defendant failed to warn about the dangers that would arise from reasonably foreseeable use of the product. Here, some sort of warning to keep it away from children or some other warning to alert children to the dangers of the product might have avoided the accident. Defendant would have an argument here that the failure to warn was not the factual and proximate case of the accident.

Note that in jurisdictions that have moved to comparative negligence, the negligence of the plaintiff may also serve as a defense to strict liability claims.

C.   Preemption analysis is two part. First, consider the statute to see if there is any language that states that the statute preempts the claim. Here, the description of the statute does not support statutory preemption. Second, consider constitutional preemption based on a conflict between the statute and its policies and the state common law cause of action. Usually, the federal policy of uniformity supports finding preemption. Here, the federal statute mandates that product tie-ins be safe and that safety be based on reasonableness. The statute does not conflict with a negligence cause of action, which also requires safety based on reasonableness. A harder question is whether it conflicts with strict liability-like causes of action, such as breach of warranty or the three defect-based claims. The statute's appeal to the reasonableness does seem consistent with the reasonable consumer's expectation test under breach of warranty and the equivalent reasonableness elements that can be found under each of three manufacturing defect claims. Therefore, the case can be made that there is no conflict between the federal statute and the state common law actions. Recall that it is defendants that raise the preemption argument in order to get a state cause of action dismissed. So the defendant would assert the argument that allowing reasonableness under the federal statute is inconsistent with strict liability under some common law causes of action much like the discretionary air bag standard in *Geier* conflicted with the mandatory standard that would have been imposed under the state claim for design defect. But the statute here states safety would be determined based on reasonableness, and not liability. Since even strict liability claims appeal to reasonableness for some of its elements (such as for example whether there is a design defect or whether a warning was required), the argument against preemption appears stronger.

CHECKLIST FOR PRODUCTS LIABILITY

A. The law of products liability constitutes three tort based claims: negligence, strict products liability, and misrepresentation.

B. Negligence claims have the four traditional elements: duty, breach, causation, and damages.

    1. Privity of contract was a limitation on duty in negligence claims for defective products. The famous case of MacPherson did away with the privity requirement and imposed a duty not to sell a product negligently made regardless of lack of contract.

    2. Unreasonable conduct is established by showing that the defendant engaged in conduct that fell below the standard of care, using the methods of showing breach discussed in Chapter Four.

C. Strict products liability claims hold the seller of a defective product liable for physical harm to purchasers or users and their product without regard to fault on the part of the seller.

    1. Strict product liability has its roots in the law of warranties and in the application of strict liability to ultrahazardous activities.

    2. The key issue in a strict products liability case is whether a product is defective. There are three types of defects.

        a. Manufacturing defect: the product was made incorrectly in the factory. This type of defect is shown by the product not functioning as expected.

      b. Design defect: the product was designed in an improper way. This is shown through either the consumer expectations test or the risk-utility test.

      c. Warning defect: the seller failed to warn about dangers that they knew or should have known about. The warning must be informative to a reasonable consumer to be adequate.

  3. A product whose inherent characteristics are dangerous is not defective.

D. Misrepresentation is another claim that is brought as part of a products liability cause of action. The elements of misrepresentation are presented in Chapter Thirteen.

E. Special defenses in products liability cases: the defenses for negligence and strict liability claims discussed in Chapter Nine apply to products liability. In addition, there are special defenses to also keep in mind.

  1. Not a product: strict product liability claims do not apply to the sale of services or of land.

  2. State of the art: for design defect claims, the defendant can point to the state of technology at the time a product was made to defend against a claim of defective design. Some jurisdictions reject this defense on the ground that sellers of products need to keep up with developments in technology.

  3. Conduct of the consumer: improper usage and modifications by the user can be a defense to product liability claims.

  4. Other property rule: a defect that keeps a product for functioning but does not harm other property or cause personal injury is not a basis for a product liability claim.

  5. Preemption: if a state tort claim imposes a standard in conflict with a federal standard, then the federal standard trumps.

      (i) Express preemption: a federal statute or regulation expressly states that a state tort claim cannot be brought.

(ii) Implied preemption: ask if a federal statute or regulation creates a safety standard. Then ask if a state tort claim creates a standard inconsistent with the federal standard. If the state tort claim does create an inconsistent standard, then the state tort claim is dismissed.

(iii) Do not confuse the defense of preemption with the use of statutes to establish negligence per se.

F. Restatement (Third) of Torts: Products Liability

1. Adopted more than half the states.: a dynamic area so pay attention to your particular instructor about developments.

2. Manufacturing defect: strict liability if product does not conform to intended design.

3. Design defect: risk-utility test is the sole one with customer expectations relevant to determining risk or utility of design. Plaintiff must show reasonable alternative design unless design is "manifestly unreasonable."

4. Inadequate warning or instruction: foreseeable risk could have been avoided or mitigated through reasonable warning or instructions, where reasonableness depends on the circumstances.

CHAPTER 12

Reputation Based Torts

GENERAL APPROACH

The reputation based torts include defamation and the four torts protecting privacy: false light, public disclosure of private facts, intrusion, and right of publicity. These torts are treated separately because they involve more intangible injuries than the harms to person or to property that has largely been the focus of the torts we have discussed in the previous chapters. These torts have different elements, but share injury to personality or reputation as a common concern. In terms of standard of care, these torts illustrate a hybrid of strict liability and negligence in a way we will make clear as we explain the details of each tort. Finally, these torts also implicate constitutional issues, particularly First Amendment protections for speech and the press.

In approaching reputation based torts, you should distinguish between defamation and privacy. Within each of these, separate the common law elements of each tort from the constitutional issues. This approach explains how we structure the discussion of the torts in this chapter.

DEFAMATION

The elements of defamation are (i) a publication (ii) about the plaintiff (iii) that is defamatory which results in (iv) damages.

Defenses to defamation are (i) the truth of the statement and (ii) the statement is privileged. In addition, the defendant can raise the defense of the First Amendment under the United States Constitution. The defense of the First Amendment places a burden on the plaintiff to show that the statement was made with actual malice, if the defendant is a public official or public figure, or with fault, if the defendant is a member of the media and the plaintiff is a private person. In explaining defamation, we will first go through the four elements of plaintiff's case and then discuss the defenses.

Plaintiff's case for defamation

<u>Publication</u>: The plaintiff must establish that the communication was communicated, either orally or in writing, to a third party, other than the plaintiff or the defendant. For liability to attach, the communication has to have been sent intentionally or negligently. Review the definition of intent from Chapter Two. To show that a publication was sent negligently, the plaintiff must show that the defendant acted unreasonably in letting the communication be published. Review the ways that a plaintiff can establish unreasonable conduct from Chapter Four. All of them apply here, except for *res ipsa loquitur* and the use of statutes. Note that if a defendant simply says something defamatory to a plaintiff directly and no third party hears or receives the defendant's statement, then there is no publication and no basis for defamation.

An author, a publisher, or a distributor (or all three) can be held liable for defamation. Liability for an author or a publisher is strict liability unless the First Amendment rules apply (see below). Liability for a distributor (such as a bookseller or a newspaper vendor) is based on negligence. Do not be confused about the standard of care. For all defendants, the publication must have been either intentional or negligent. But once the plaintiff establishes the publication requirement, the plaintiff must also establish that a distributor was negligent in distributing the defamatory statement. This means that the distributor knew or should have known about the defamatory content of the publication it is distributing. For an author or a publisher of the communication, however, the plaintiff need only show that the defamatory communication was published intentionally or negligently. The author or publisher need not know that the communication itself is defamatory or intend that the statement is defamatory. Liability is strict in that sense. As we will discuss below, the constitutional defense adds certain requirements for the plaintiff to establish a case for defamation.

Under federal law, an Internet service provider is immune from a defamation suit based on a statement made by someone using the service to post online. The purpose of this immunity is to protect the Internet service provider from excessive lawsuits that could arise from the high traffic of communications made on the Internet.

About the plaintiff: The communication need not name the plaintiff for the plaintiff to establish a defamation claim. If the plaintiff can establish the identity of the subject of the communication through context, then this element is satisfied. However, general statements about groups cannot be the basis for a defamation claim unless the group is fairly small and individual members of the group can be readily identified. For example, statements about a religious or ethnic group cannot be a basis for defamation if they are generally about the group. A statement such as "all workers at X law firm" are corrupt may be. Furthermore, a statement about a corporate entity can give rise to a defamation action by the corporate entity or by identifiable members of that entity if they can be identified. For example, the statement "X Corporation is a really badly run company" can give rise to a defamation action by the corporation and by the managers of the corporation, whose managerial skills are being impugned.

Defamatory: The plaintiff must show that the statement is harmful to one's reputation. The statement can be harmful to one's personal or professional standing in the community. In determining whether a statement is defamatory, a court will look at the statement literally and use background context to determine how a reasonable person would understand the statement. For example, the statement "X did not go to medical school" would be defamatory if X holds himself out as a prominent member of the medical profession but harmless if X is an attorney who never made any claims to have gone to medical school. As another example, the statement "X was seen going into 123 Maple Street" is defamatory if 123 Maple Street is a known residence for drug dealers and prostitutes, but not if 123 Maple Street is a private residence where X lives. Whether a statement is defamatory depends on a reasonable person standard, which is an appeal to the community in which the defamation suit is being brought.

Damages: This element is the most tricky and the most important part of a defamation claim. This element depends upon whether the communication was spoken (called slander) or written (called libel).

If the communication was spoken, then the plaintiff must show special damages in order to have a claim for defamation. Special damages mean specific monetary loss that resulted from the spoken communication. There are four types of slander, however, for which damages are presumed and the plaintiff need not show special damages. These four cases of slander per se are: (i) a statement that the plaintiff had engaged in a serious crime; (ii) a statement injurious to the plaintiff's trade, business, or profession; (iii) a statement that the plaintiff has a loathsome disease; or (iv) a statement imputing lack of chastity in a woman. Some states have modified or eliminated these categories of slander per se, particularly the fourth one. To repeat, if the slander does not fit into one of these categories, then the plaintiff has to show special damages.

If the communication was written, then most jurisdictions will presume damages. The plaintiff need not show special damages. Some states, however, require a plaintiff to show damages for libel unless (i) the statement is defamatory on its face or (ii) the statement fits into one of the categories of slander per se listed above. These states are in the minority. Within these minority states, a statement is defamatory on its face if the defamatory meaning can be inferred without extrinsic evidence to interpret the statement. These minority states use the terminology libel per se to refer to libelous statements that do not require the plaintiff to show special damages and libel per quod to refer to libelous statement that do require the plaintiff to show special damages.

Defenses to defamation

There are three principal defenses to defamation: (i) truth; (ii) privileged communication; and (iii) First Amendment.

Truth: The defendant can point to the truth of a statement as a complete defense to the claim of defamation. Some states have required absolute truth as a defense, meaning that even an iota of falsity would remove the defense. For example, if the statement is "X did not go to medical school," the truth of this statement would be a defense to defamation. Suppose, however, that the statement made was "X, whose hair is red, did not go to medical school." In some states that require absolute truth, if X's hair was not red, then the truth defense would be lost even if the part of the medical school were true. Most states require substantial truth for the defense to be successful so that some inconsequential false statements within a true one would not eliminate the defense.

Privileged statement: Some statements are subject to absolute privilege. Such statements include ones made by a public official in their public capacity or sworn testimony. The purpose of this privilege is to allow official communications to be made without the fear of a defamation suit. Some statements are subject to a qualified privilege, which means that the statements are immune from forming the basis for liability if they are made and used for the purpose intended. An example of a qualified privilege would be a reference by an employer for a former employee or by a professor for a student. In such contexts, the statement is made for the purposes of communicating one's views about a candidate, and the qualified privilege allows the communication to be made without the fear of a lawsuit. However, any privilege can be lost if the person making the communicating exceeds the scope of the privilege. To defeat the privilege, the plaintiff must show that the statement was made with malice, that is with an intent to harm the plaintiff or with reckless disregard for the truth or falsity of the statement made.

First Amendment: In *New York Times v. Sullivan*, 376 U.S. 254 (1964), the Supreme Court held that the First Amendment applied to a defamation cause of action. The First Amendment protects against the abridgment of speech by Congress, and through incorporation in the Fourteenth Amendment by state government. In its *Sullivan* decision, the Supreme Court held that a public official bringing a defamation suit had to show that the defamatory statement was made with actual malice, meaning that the defendant knew that the statement was false or the defendant acted with reckless disregard to the falsity of the statement. In subsequent cases, the Supreme Court extended this requirement to public figures bringing defamation claims. A public figure is someone who has public prominence or has public attention cast upon them because of some famous act.

The Supreme Court has also addressed the issue of how the First Amendment applies to a defamation suit brought by a private person. In *Gertz v. Robert Welch, Inc,* 418 U.S. 323 (1974), the Court held that it is unconstitutional to impose strict liability on a media defendant in a defamation suit brought by a private person. The rationale of this ruling is to protect the First Amendment interests of media defendants. In most states, a private plaintiff must show that a media defendant acted negligently in making a defamatory statement. Some states require a showing of intent.

To understand the role of the First Amendment in altering defamation law, consider the following summary of the rules.

Private plaintiff suing non-media defendant must show:

- Publication made intentionally or negligently

- About plaintiff

- Defamatory statement (negligently made if defendant is distributor; strict liability otherwise)

- Damages

Public Official or Public Figure suing any defendant must show:

- Publication made intentionally or negligently

- About plaintiff

- Defamatory statement made with actual malice

- Damages

Private plaintiff suing media defendant must show:

- Publication made intentionally or negligently

- About plaintiff

- Defamatory statement made intentionally or negligently

- Damages

PRIVACY

The privacy torts were developed by courts in the early part of the Twentieth Century in response to concerns over intrusions into the private sphere by private persons and the media. Tort law protects this private space through four causes of action. Each cause of action illustrates issues of the standard of care and the role of the First Amendment in protecting speech interests.

False Light: A plaintiff has a cause of action against a defendant for false light if the defendant portrays the plaintiff in a way that would create a false impression to a reasonable person viewing the communication. The cause of action has much in common with the defamation claim except that the communication need not be defamatory; it must only be false. The Supreme Court has held that the First Amendment is a defense to a false light claim if the communication is of a matter of public concern. If the defendant can show that the communication is a matter of public concern, then the plaintiff must show actual malice, that is the defendant either knew of the falsity or made the statement with reckless disregard for the truth.

Public Disclosure of Private Facts: A plaintiff has a claim against a defendant for the public disclosure of private facts if the defendant (i) publicizes a matter concerning the private life of the plaintiff, (ii) where the matter publicized would be highly offensive to a reasonable person, and (iii) the matter is not of legitimate concern to the public. Consent of the plaintiff is a defense. The defendant can be any person, whether a member of the media or a private citizen who has communicated the information to a third party. If the defendant is a member of the media, then the defendant cannot be held liable for publicizing truthful information lawfully obtained unless there is a state interest of the highest order. The Supreme Court case law deals with disclosure of the names of rape victims by newspapers when the newspaper obtained the information legally from court or police records.

Intrusion: A plaintiff has a claim against a defendant for the tort of intrusion if the defendant intentionally invades a space where the plaintiff has a reasonable expectation of privacy. Sometimes the claim might coincide with a claim for trespass to land or trespass to chattel if there is intrusion into the plaintiff's land or personal property. Often, the cases involve intrusion through electronic means into a space where the plaintiff had a reasonable expectation of being free from intrusion. The heart of the claim is the issue of reasonable expectation of privacy. This determination depends upon historical expectations as well as current community standards and the state of technology. Consent is a defense to intrusion.

If information is obtained through such intrusion, communication of that information can give rise to liability. In general, the recipient of such information is not liable. Furthermore, the gatherer of the information may have protection under the First Amendment if there is a strong public interest in knowing the information. The First Amendment protection rests on a balance between the privacy interests in being free from invasion with the interest of the public in knowing the information that was obtained.

Right of publicity: A plaintiff has a claim against a defendant for violation of the right of publicity if the defendant commercializes the name, likeness, or other personal attribute of the plaintiff without the plaintiff's consent. Cases have expanded what is protected under the right of publicity to include voice, one's celebrity image, a catchphrase, and items associated with one's public image, such as a race car or a cape. The earliest case to raise a right of publicity claim lead to a rejection by the court because of concerns with the First Amendment. The Supreme Court has not found a First Amendment defense to a right of publicity claim, and in the only case to raise the First Amendment issue, the Court held that the First Amendment was not a defense if the defendant undermined the full commercial value of the plaintiff's publicity. Lower courts have protected First Amendment values in cases involving works that incorporated the image of a celebrity. In a famous case involving a celebratory portrait of Tiger Woods, the court held that the right of publicity claim would not apply against a work that transformed the public image in a creative way. The court relied on an earlier case that found a right of publicity claim against a defendant that simply took the images of The Three Stooges and placed them on a t-shirt. This use of the images was found not to be transformative or creative.

Problems. The problems on this material are part of the "Example of a Comprehensive Exam" at the end of the book.

CHECKLIST FOR REPUTATION BASED TORTS

A. The reputation based torts consist of defamation and four individual tort claims that fall under protection of privacy.

B. Defamation: (i) publication (ii) about the plaintiff (iii) that is defamatory and (iv) results in damages.

    1. Publication: a communication to a third party other than plaintiff or defendant.

        a. Publication must have been made either intentionally or negligently.

        b. If the defendant is the author or the publisher of the communication, then strict liability applies to the other elements of the defamation claim.

        c. If the defendant is the distributor of the communication, then the distributor must have

known or should have known that the communication was defamatory.

d. Under federal law, Internet service providers
have immunity from defamation claims based
on defamatory communications made by users
of the service.

2. About the plaintiff

a. The subject of the communication can be apparent from the literal words of the communication or from the context of the
communication.

b. Group defamation is possible if the individuals
who comprise the group are specific and easily
ascertainable. General statements about groups
are not actionable as defamation.

3. Defamatory: based on a reasonable interpretation of the
communication.

4. Damages: depends on the nature of the communication.

a. If spoken (that is slander), then special damages must be shown unless the communication
falls into one of four slander per se categories:

i.   Serious criminal conduct.

ii. Harm to trade, business, or
profession.

iii. Loathsome disease.

iv. Unchastity of a woman.

b. In most jurisdictions, if the communication is
written (libel), then general damages are presumed and special damages need not be shown.

c. In some jurisdictions, special damages are required for libel unless

i.   the statement is defamatory on its
face OR

ii. the statement counts as slander per
se.

      d. In these latter jurisdictions, libel requiring the showing of special damages is referred to as libel per quod and libel not requiring the showing of special damages is referred to as libel per se.

  5. Defenses to defamation

      a. Truth: generally a substantial truth standard.

      b. Privileges:

          i. Absolute for public officials and official statements.

          ii. Qualified for references and other contexts in which truthful and open communication is desirable.

          iii. If the defendant has malice, then the privilege is lost.

      c. First Amendment: imposes an additional requirement on the plaintiff

          i. Defendant is public official or public figure: plaintiff must show that defendant has actual malice, i.e. that defendant knew of the falsity of the communication or acted with reckless disregard for its falsity.

          ii. Defendant is from the media and the plaintiff is a private person: liability cannot be strict. Most jurisdictions require the plaintiff to show that the media defendant acted negligently in making the defamatory communication. Some jurisdictions require intent.

C. Privacy torts

  1. False light: defendant published a statement about the plaintiff that was false.

      a. If the communication is a matter of public concern, then the plaintiff must show actual malice.

2. Public Disclosure of private facts: defendant (i) publicizes a matter concerning the private life of the plaintiff, (ii) where the matter publicized would be highly offensive to a reasonable person, and (iii) the matter is not of legitimate concern to the public.

    a. Consent of the plaintiff is a defense.

    b. If defendant is a member of the media, then there can be no liability for the publication of truthful information legally obtained unless the state has an interest of the highest order.

3. Intrusion: defendant intentionally intrudes in a place where the plaintiff has a reasonable expectation of privacy.

    a. Consent of the plaintiff is a defense.

    b. If the defendant communicates information obtained from the intrusion, then the defendant has a First Amendment defense if the public interest in the information outweighs the privacy concerns of the plaintiff.

    c. A third party who obtains the information from the defendant is not liable.

4. Right of publicity: defendant commercializes the name, likeness or other personal attribute of the plaintiff.

    a. The Supreme Court has held that there is no First Amendment defense if the defendant takes all commercial value of the plaintiff's publicity.

    b. Lower courts have found First Amendment protection if the defendant transforms the public attribute of the plaintiff in a creative manner.

CHAPTER 13

Business Torts

GENERAL APPROACH

Your Torts class may cover the subject of Business Torts towards the very end of the course, if at all. The legal regulation of business is discussed in contract law and perhaps in your first year property class. Some of the more substantive business torts are dealt with in more advanced courses such as Business Organizations, Securities, and Intellectual Property. The business torts you might cover in your Torts class are the basic ones. They can be divided into two categories: those that deal with information in a business relationship and those that deal with interferences with business relationships, both formal ones involving contract and informal ones. In analyzing each tort, focus on the elements and the main issues raised by the particular elements.

MISREPRESENTATION

A plaintiff can sue a defendant for false statements made by the defendant that resulted in harm to the plaintiff. Misrepresentation can be either intentional (which is referred to as fraud or deceit) or negligent (which is referred to as negligent misrepresentation.)

The elements of fraud, or deceit, are: (i) a material misrepresentation by the defendant; (ii) the defendant acted with the requisite scienter; (iii) the defendant intended to induce reliance; (iv) the misrepresentation caused the plaintiff's justifiable reliance; (v) pecuniary damages resulted to the plaintiff.

The elements of negligent misrepresentation are: (i) a material misrepresentation by the defendant; (ii) the defendant acted unreasonably in disclosing or investigating the facts represented; (iii) the misrepresentation caused the plaintiff's reasonable and justifiable reliance; (iv) pecuniary damages to the plaintiff.

It is worth comparing these elements. Both types of misrepresentation require a material misrepresentation. Material means that a reasonable person entering into the transaction would think the information is important to the decision. The misrepresentation has to be one of fact, but a statement of opinion will be treated as one of fact if it comes from someone who holds himself out as having the requisite expertise in the field.

For a claim of fraud or deceit, the defendant must have scienter, meaning that the defendant either knew that the statement was false or acted with reckless disregard to the statement's falsity. For a claim of negligent misrepresentation, the defendant must have acted below the standard of reasonable care in the field in making the representation or in investigating the truth or falsity of the statement.

A claim of fraud or deceit requires that the defendant intended to induce requirement. No showing of intent is required for the negligent misrepresentation claim.

Both types of misrepresentation claim require a showing of reliance. A plaintiff must show that the misrepresentation caused the plaintiff to enter the transaction. For the fraud or deceit claim, the reliance must be justified, meaning that the plaintiff had no other basis to know that the statement was false. There is in general no duty on the part of the plaintiff to investigate a statement. But if a statement is obviously false, then the reliance will not be justified. For a negligent misrepresentation claim, the reliance must be reasonable as well as justified. Reasonable reliance means that a reasonable person involved in the same transaction as the plaintiff would have relied on the misstatement.

Both types of misrepresentation can remedy the same types of damages: monetary harm to the plaintiff and any physical harm suffered. Punitive damages are available for fraud or deceit, but not for negligent misrepresentation. Finally, a plaintiff can rescind a transaction if there was fraud or deceit, but not if the misrepresentation was negligent.

INJURIOUS FALSEHOOD

This tort is also referred to as disparagement and covers false and harmful statements made about someone's business or products, as opposed to someone's personal reputation. Such a statement may, by inference, also be the basis for a defamation claim. If a person says that the X Company makes shoddy products, that statement may be the basis for a defamation claim. But a defamation claim does not necessarily follow from a disparagement. For example, suppose someone says: "X is a great company, but their new brand is a really shoddy one." That statement says negative things about the product, but not necessarily about the company.

The elements of injurious falsehood are: (i) a false statement of a kind calculated to damage a pecuniary interest of the plaintiff; (ii) publication to a third party; (iii) malice in the publication; and (iv) special damages suffered by the plaintiff. Although this tort, like defamation, implicates First Amendment issues, no separate First Amendment analysis has developed for this tort because the elements are quite difficult to show. Consequently, the tort creates liability for a very narrow range of statements and for statements that are of questionable value under the First Amendment. The plaintiff must show that the statement is "calculated to damage a pecuniary interest," that the defendant showed malice in publishing the statement, and that special damages resulted. These three elements make the claim apply to harmful speech as opposed to statements that might be made in media coverage or reporting.

INTENTIONAL INTERFERENCE WITH CONTRACTS

The elements of this tort are: (i) existence of a valid contract; (ii) knowledge of the valid contract by the defendant; (iii) intent by the defendant to interfere with the valid contract; (iv) interference with the contract caused by the defendant; and (v) damages to the plaintiff. The defendant can defend against this claim by showing justification for the interference such as (i) the nature of the defendant's conduct; (ii) the defendant's motive; (iii) the interests of the third party with which the defendant's conduct interferes; (iv) the interests sought to be advanced by the defendant; (v) the social interests in protecting the freedom of action of the defendant and the contractual or economic interests of the third party; (vi) the proximity or remoteness of the defendant's conduct to the interference; and (vii) the relations between the parties. Note that punitive damages are available for intentional interference with contract and intentional interference with economic relations (the next and last tort).

INTENTIONAL INTERFERENCE WITH ECONOMIC RELATIONS

This tort is analogous to intentional interference with contract except for the lack of a valid contractual relationship. The elements of this tort are: (i) existence of an economic relationship between the plaintiff and a third party that has the possibility of resulting in future economic gain to the plaintiff; (ii) knowledge by the defendant of the existence of the relationship; (iii) intent by the defendant to interfere with the economic relationship; (iv) actual interference; and (v) damages to the plaintiff caused by the interference. The defenses discussed under intentional interference with contract apply to this tort as well.

MISAPPROPRIATION

This final tort has its roots in the Supreme Court's decision in *International News Service v. Associated Press*, 248 U.S. 215 (1918). At issue in the case was the copying of the news by International News Service from Associated Press, a news agency that had expended time and money in gathering and researching the news. The Supreme Court held that Associated Press had a quasi-property right in the news that allowed the company to enjoin a competitor from copying it. Justice Holmes' famous concurrence reasoned that the quasi-property right is time-limited and the injunction should have a short duration. Justice Brandeis' equally famous dissent argued against a property right as being in conflict with federal intellectual property law, which did not give protection to factual information, like the news.

The holding of the *Associated Press* case has been questioned. The contemporary view of the tort of misappropriation is provided by the Second Circuit's decision in *National Basketball Association v. Motorola, Inc.*, 105 F.3d 841 (1997), which laid out the following five elements to the claim of misappropriation: (i) Plaintiff gathered information at a cost; (ii) Information is time sensitive; (iii) Defendant's use constitutes free riding of plaintiff's effort; (iv) Plaintiff and defendant are direct competitors; and (v) Defendant's free riding would substantially reduce the incentive of plaintiff to gather the information.

Problems. The problems on this material are integrated into the "Example of a Comprehensive Exam" at the end of the book.

CHECKLIST FOR BUSINESS TORTS

A. Misrepresentation: can be intentional or negligent.

    1. Fraud or deceit: (i) a material misrepresentation; (ii) the defendant acted with the requisite scienter; (iii) the defendant intended to induce reliance; (iv) the misrepresentation caused the plaintiff's justifiable reliance; (v) pecuniary damages resulted to the plaintiff.

        a. Fraud or deceit can be the basis for damages or rescission.

    2. Negligent misrepresentation: (i) a material misrepresentation; (ii) the defendant acted unreasonably in disclosing or investigating the facts represented; (iii) the misrepresentation caused the plaintiff's reasonable and justifiable reliance; (iv) pecuniary damages to the plaintiff.

        a. Negligent misrepresentation is remedied by damages.

B. Injurious Falsehood: (i) a false statement of a kind calculated to damage a pecuniary interest of the plaintiff; (ii) publication to a third party; (iii) malice in the publication; and (iv) special damages suffered by the plaintiff.

C. Intentional Interference with Contract: (i) existence of a valid contract; (ii) knowledge of the valid contract by the defendant; (iii) intent by the defendant to interfere with the valid contract; (iv) interference with the contract caused by the defendant; and (v) damages to the plaintiff.

    1. Justifications: (i) the nature of the defendant's conduct; (ii) the defendant's motive; (iii) the interests of the third party with which the defendant's conduct interferes; (iv) the interests sought to be advanced by the defendant; (v) the social interests in protecting the freedom of action of the defendant and the contractual or economic interests of the third party; (vi) the proximity or remoteness of the defendant's conduct to the interference; and (vii) the relations between the parties.

D. Intentional Interference with Economic Relations: (i) existence of an economic relationship between the plaintiff and a third party that has the possibility of resulting in future economic gain to the plaintiff; (ii) knowledge by the defendant of the existence of the relationship; (iii) intent by the defendant to interfere with the economic relationship; (iv) actual interference; and (v) damages to the plaintiff caused by the interference.

    1. Justifications: same as under intentional interference with contract.

E. Misappropriation: this tort consists of the following five elements to the claim of misappropriation: (i) Plaintiff gathered information at a cost; (ii) Information is time sensitive; (iii) Defendant's use constitutes free riding of plaintiff's effort; (iv) Plaintiff and defendant are direct competitors; and (v) Defendant's free riding would substantially reduce the incentive of plaintiff to gather the information.

CHAPTER 14

Torts Arising From the Legal Process

GENERAL APPROACH

A defendant who is found not liable in a tort or other civil action (or not guilty in a criminal prosecution) can bring a suit for malicious institution of civil proceedings (or malicious prosecution). In addition, if someone is hurt by a the misuse of a legal proceeding (such as a subpoena or an attachment of property), then the victim can bring a claim for abuse of process. As you can imagine, a lawsuit to vindicate a lawsuit can lead to the propagation of litigation. The standards for bringing a tort claim arising from the legal process are consequently quite high.

The torts discussed in this chapter should be compared with a Rule 11 sanction under the Federal Rules for Civil Procedure (and comparable rules under state law). A Rule 11 sanction is not a tort claim, but a penalty that can be imposed by a judge in a civil proceeding to punish a litigant who has submitted a frivolous pleading. The standards for a Rule 11 sanction are presented below.

MALICIOUS INSTITUTION OF CIVIL PRO-CEEDINGS

A claim for malicious institution of civil proceedings is considered an intent based tort and has five elements. The plaintiff in the malicious institution proceeding must show the following: (1) bringing a civil proceeding against the plaintiff; (2) termination of the proceeding in favor of the plaintiff; (3) absence of a reasonable basis for the proceeding; (4) improper purpose of the party bringing the proceeding; and (5) damages suffered by the plaintiff.

There are several points to emphasize about the individual elements. First, the original civil proceeding must have been terminated resulting in a finding in favor of the party bring the malicious institution proceeding. If the original suit settled, then there is no basis for the second suit. The party bringing the second suit need have prevailed on all the claims in the first suit.

Second, the third element has both an objective and a subjective component. In order to establish the third element, the party bringing the malicious institution claim has to show that there was no objective basis for the claim in the original suit and that there was no subjective basis for the plaintiff who brought the original suit. If the plaintiff in the original suit had a good faith belief that his claim was valid, then the party bringing the malicious institution claim has failed to establish the claim.

Third, the party bringing the malicious prosecution suit has to show that the plaintiff in the original suit had an improper purpose in bringing the claim. Improper purpose is sometimes also referred to as malice. The concept refers to a purpose for bringing the original lawsuit other than the vindication of legally protected rights. This primary purpose could be harassment of the other party or vindictiveness. Hatred of or animosity towards the other party is not enough. However, note that this third element is distinct from the second. If the plaintiff in the original law suit had a primary purpose to harass but also subjectively believed the party was liable (and there was an objective basis for the claim), then the party bringing the malicious institution claim will not prevail. These requirements and their interplay should give you a sense of how difficult it is to succeed in these torts arising from the legal process.

Finally, the party bringing the malicious institution proceeding can recover damages that resulted from the original suit. There is a strict causation requirement, and the party will most likely recover injury to reputation, emotional injury, and the costs of litigation from both suits. As of this writing, about sixteen states allow a malicious institution proceeding only if there are special damages such as seizure of the person or attachment of property. These states require special damages in order to limit this cause of action.

A claim for malicious institution of civil proceedings is different from a Rule 11 sanction under the Federal Rules for Civil Procedure (and analogous state laws). A Rule 11 sanction is imposed by a judge within a civil proceeding upon motion of a party. The sanction is meant to punish an attorney for filing a frivolous pleading, motion or other document. When an attorney files a pleading, motion, or other document, he or she must sign it. This signature warrants the following under Rule 11(b):

"(1) [the pleading, motion, or document] is not being presented for any improper purpose, such as to harass, cause unnecessary delay, or needlessly increase the cost of litigation;

"(2) the claims, defenses, and other legal contentions are warranted by existing law or by a nonfrivolous argument for extending, modifying, or reversing existing law or for establishing new law;

"(3) the factual contentions have evidentiary support or, if specifically so identified, will likely have evidentiary support after a reasonable opportunity for further investigation or discovery; and

"(4) the denials of factual contentions are warranted on the evidence or, if specifically so identified, are reasonably based on belief or a lack of information."

If the moving party can show that the filed document fails to meet one or more of these representations, the judge can impose a monetary sanction against the filing attorney. Notice that a Rule 11 sanction can be brought against either the plaintiff's attorney or the defendant's.

MALICIOUS PROSECUTION

A claim for malicious prosecution has the same elements as a claim for malicious institution for civil proceedings: (1) bringing a civil proceeding against the plaintiff; (2) termination of the proceeding in favor of the plaintiff; (3) absence of probable cause for the proceeding; (4) improper purpose of the party bringing the proceeding; and (5) damages suffered by the plaintiff.

One difference is in element (3) reflecting the probable cause requirement for bringing a criminal prosecution. The key difference is that the original suit giving rise to the malicious prosecution claim is a criminal case. This difference is critical, however, because of the existence of immunity for state actors and judicial actors. This immunity means that absent a waiver, police officers, judges, prosecutors, witnesses, and other judicial officers cannot be sued for a malicious prosecution claim. Often, the claim is brought against the individual who brought the criminal complaint leading up to the prosecution. However, if the state actor or judicial actor was acting outside the scope of their duties, for example by fabricating physical evidence or suborning perjury, then the immunity will be lost.

ABUSE OF PROCESS

Both of the previous two torts require the termination of a civil or criminal proceeding in favor of the accused before the tort claim can be pursued. However, a party may be subject to abuse of the legal process before the termination of a proceeding or despite lack of success a trial. For example, a party might subpoena an individual simply to harass them. Or an individual might be subjected to false arrest and imprisonment. In some of these cases, the injured party might raise the claim of false imprisonment or some other tort. In general, the tort claim of abuse of process allows a party to obtain recovery for damages arising from the use of legal process brought for an improper purpose. The elements of such a claim are: (1) initiating a legal process, such as an attachment or an arrest; (2) absence of a reasonable basis for the proceeding; (3) improper purpose of the party bringing the proceeding; and (4) damages suffered by the plaintiff.

■ PROBLEM ■

For over the decade, Frank owned the only hardware store on Main Street. A year ago, Joe opened a new hardware store across the street from Frank's. Frank was concerned about the competition. He did notice that Joe's store was not in compliance with a zoning ordinance on the amount of the sidewalk that had to be set aside in front of commercial establishments. Frank told the zoning board about this possible violation, and the board fined Joe according to the criminal code for zoning violations as a misdemeanor. Frank also told Jim, Joe's neighbor, to check the boundary lines of Joe's store because there might be trespass. Jim did check and found that Joe had built his store onto Jim's property. Jim subsequently brought a trespass action that Joe was able to win. There was no appeal. Joe also went to a hearing of the zoning board and was able to have the fines repealed after obtaining a variance for the zoning violation.

Joe has found out about Frank's reports and brings a claim of malicious institution, malicious prosecution, and abuse of process against Jim and Frank. Analyze the likely result of Joe's claims

Suggested Answer

Joe v. Jim

Jim is likely to prevail. Although there is a completed civil litigation that came out in favor of Joe, Joe will have a hard time showing a lack of basis for Jim's claims and improper purpose of Jim's part. The facts state that Jim checked the boundary lines and thought there was a trespass. Unfortunately he was wrong, but the boundary line records and his inspection would support an objective and subjective bases for his claim of trespass against Joe. Furthermore, while Jim was informed by Frank to check the boundary lines, it does not seem that Jim was motivated by any purpose other than to assert what he thought was his legal right. The third and fourth elements will pose a problem for Joe's claim against Jim.

Joe v. Frank

Frank did not sue Joe. So Joe's claim would not be for malicious institutional of a civil proceeding, but for malicious prosecution or abuse of process. As for the malicious prosecution claim, there would be a question of whether an administrative proceeding brought before an entity like the zoning board would count as criminal prosecution. The board seemingly can impose criminal-like penalties, but the proceeding is administrative, not criminal. Furthermore, there would be an issue as whether there was probable cause for the acts of the zoning board. The facts suggest there might be. But the reversal of the fines suggests that the basis might be in doubt. In addition, although Frank did not like the competition from Joe's store, it seemed that Frank was not motivated solely by a desire to harass or harm Joe's business. So, Joe may have a hard time showing improper purpose on Frank's part.

Joe's abuse of process claim against Frank would suffer from the same problems regarding the basis for the claim and Frank's improper purpose. But there need not be a completed proceeding for this claim to be successful. Instead, Frank's informing the board of a possible zoning violation would count as the initiation of a legal process, meeting the first element of the claim for abuse of process.

 CHECKLIST FOR TORTS ARISING FROM THE LEGAL PROCESS

A. Malicious Initiation of Civil Proceedings

    1. Elements: (1) bringing a civil proceeding against the plaintiff; (2) termination of the proceeding in favor of the plaintiff; (3) absence of a reasonable basis for the proceeding; (4) improper purpose of the party bringing the proceeding; and (5) damages suffered by the plaintiff.

    2. Different from Rule 11 Sanctions which are penalties

imposed by a judge in a civil proceeding against an attorney who has submitted a frivolous or fraudulent pleading, motion, or other document.

B. Malicious Prosecution

1. Elements: (1) bringing a civil proceeding against the plaintiff; (2) termination of the proceeding in favor of the plaintiff; (3) absence of probable cause for the proceeding; (4) improper purpose of the party bringing the proceeding; and (5) damages suffered by the plaintiff.

2. Existence of immunities will limit the suit.

C. Abuse of Process

1. Elements: (1) initiating a legal process, such as an attachment or an arrest; (2) absence of a reasonable basis for the proceeding; (3) improper purpose of the party bringing the proceeding; and (4) damages suffered by the plaintiff.

Exam Pointers

Here are some pointers to help you through the final examination for the course. This book should help you in reviewing most of the materials you have covered in the course. There may be a few topics that this book does not cover but your Torts class did. Keep in mind that this book is a study aid and not a substitute for your class. Look to your class syllabus, casebook, and class notes first in preparing for the final. Use this book as a supplement to those materials.

- Review the materials:

    - Look to your syllabus, casebook and class notes to see what topics your professor covered over the semester.

    - Make sure you know what points were covered in class.

    - Use this study guide to clarify and organize the main points you covered in class.

    - Start an outline based on your class materials and the checklists provided in this study guide. The checklists at the end of each chapter have been collected as an outline at the end of the book.

- Preparing for the exam:

    - Put together an outline for the course based on your class materials and the checklists in this study guide.

- Based on the materials covered in your class, identify the issues you are likely to see on the exam.

- For each issue, work through your approach on how to analyze and write about the issue using the facts that you will see on the exam.

- Use this study guide to help you recognize the issues and how to work through them.

- Use the problems in this book and old exams from your course to get used to fact patterns and how to analyze them.

- During the exam:

  - Stay calm and recognize that these are a just a few hours during which you need to focus on the subject of Torts.

  - Read the question thoroughly. Start with the end to identify what you are being asked by your professor. Then proceed through the facts.

  - Take notes as you read to identify the issues that you see.

  - Organize the reading notes to see how your final answer will be organized. Pick a form of organization: either by party or by tort.

  - For each tort that you see, state the elements and then discuss the elements that are at issue in the facts you are given.

  - Integrate discussion of facts with their relevance to the legal issue.

  - Structure your answer into paragraphs so that someone who is reading your answer will know what you are taking about.

  - Have the outline you have created nearby so that you can refer to it quickly if necessary. If closed book exam, have the outline memorized in as concise a manner as possible.

- Remember you are in charge during the exam and the more you have prepared beforehand, the more in charge you will be.

- After the exam:

  - Take a breath, don't talk to others about the exam, and try to forget about it.

  - Move on to the next exam.

  - If Torts is your last exam, congratulations! Take a break from law school for a while, but be ready to get back into things next semester. Enjoy a job well done!

Example of a Comprehensive Exam

Followed by a Detailed Memo on Exam Taking

Exam Question

Shelly Levene and Ricky Roma are two competing realtors in the city of Sprawl. They have each worked in the areas of commercial and residential real estate in Sprawl for ten years and have grown to be bitter rivals. Ricky Roma's business is perhaps the more profitable one in the city largely because of his aggressive advertising campaign, which consists largely of bulletin board and web advertising targeted to the residential end of the market. The ads depict Ricky Roma and members of his real family standing around the family Volvo and contain the catch phrase: "Ricky Roma—the realtor to come to for family values".

The following facts serve as the basis for a lawsuit initiated by Shelly against Ricky. In January 2004, Shelly undertook a large commercial real estate project with an out-of-state developer with plans to build a mega-shopping mall at the outskirts of Sprawl. The developer had detailed architectural plans and a confidential business plan that he had given to Shelly under a confidentiality agreement. In mid February, Shelly noticed that the files containing the plans were out of place and suspected that Tony, a recently hired temporary employee, had tampered with the files. Shelly investigated Tony's background and discovered that he was Ricky Roma's nephew. She suspected that Ricky was using Tony to spy on Shelly's business and learn more about the shopping mall project, whose completion would increase land values in the area outside Sprawl. Shelly fired Tony and retained a private investigator to research Ricky's activities.

At the end of March, the private investigator submitted a report to Shelly. The report stated that a corporation had been buying up land around the site for the planned shopping mall in late January. The corporation was formed by two individuals who were connected to Ricky Roma although Ricky did not have any direct involvement with either the formation of the corporation or the land transactions. In addition, the report stated that all was not peaceful in the Roma household. Conversations with the Roma's neighbors revealed that they frequently heard shouting and screaming coming from the Roma household and that Mrs. Roma often appeared at neighborhood functions with strange bruises on her face, which were attributed to accidents. Finally, the report stated that Ricky Roma would often be away from home during the weekends and that the Roma family Volvo, depicted in Roma's ads, could be found in the parking lot of out of the way hotels located at the outskirts of Sprawl. After receiving the report, Shelly terminated the investigator's services and kept the report under lock and key in her office.

April and May were typically busy months for residential real estate in Sprawl, but business seemed to be down for Ricky during those months in 2004. He thought it was perhaps the downturn in the economy, but he became suspicious when at a local realtors' convention in May, he received the cold shoulder from several clients. When he shared his concerns with a colleague at the convention, Ricky was told to look at his web site. Logging onto the site from his hotel room, he found that someone had tampered with his site and had changed his catchphrase to read "Are these family values?" The doctored site went on to list the following statements: "Do family values include beating your wife? Infidelity? Lying? Cheating? Stealing other people's property?" The doctored site also included a photograph of Roma's Volvo parked outside the

Shady Acres Motel, a low rent facility on the other side of the tracks in Sprawl. Ricky immediately thought that this was Shelly's handiwork, and he made sure he would tell her what he thought about her tactics the next time he saw her. Ricky emailed an employee to take down the doctored site and left his room to look for Shelly at the convention.

Ricky eventually found Shelly with her intimate friend Lonny in the lobby of the convention hotel. In front of a crowd of about a twenty-thirty people, Ricky ran up to Shelly and berated her for doctoring his web page. Shelly and Lonny attempted to ignore him, but when Ricky ran up to Shelly's face and shouted: "Aren't you going to confess to this?," Lonny stepped in front of Shelly and tried to block Ricky. Ricky pushed Lonny violently and Lonny fell to the ground, hitting his head against the tile floor. Shelly bent over to see if Lonny was okay as the hotel security arrived and escorted Ricky away. No criminal charges were filed against Ricky or anyone else involved in the altercation.

1.   Analyze all tort claims that Shelly could raise against Ricky based on these facts. Focus on the torts and cases discussed this semester. Your answer should assess any difficulties Shelly might face in successfully bringing the claims.

2.   Analyze all tort claims that Ricky could raise against Shelly based on these facts. Focus on the torts and cases discussed this semester. Your answer should assess any difficulties Ricky might face in successfully bringing the claims.

MEMO EXPLAINING HOW TO APPROACH EXAM QUESTION

OVERVIEW OF HOW TO APPROACH EXAM

Your answer to the exam will be graded based on your ability to show that you can write and think clearly as well as apply the legal concepts discussed in class. You should spot the relevant legal issues and analyze them thoroughly based on the facts given and the law we have studied in class. The two biggest mistakes are (1) to write too much by dumping the contents of your outline and notes without attention to the subtleties of the legal issues and facts presented and (2) to write too little by jumping to conclusions, presenting one sentence answers that do no delve into the legal issues and facts presented with sufficient detail. Based on classroom discussion and one on one interactions, the latter may turn out to be the bigger problem, given the demonstrated lack of ability to think through problems in a sophisticated and well thought out way. But keep in mind that simply stating the law without any analysis or sense of how to apply the law counts for nothing.

SOME GUIDELINES

In any situation, you should spend at least half the time reading the question and organizing your answer and the rest of the time, writing your answer. Read the question at least twice: the first to acquaint yourself with what is being asked, the second to take notes on the salient issues that need to be addressed. Once you have done the preliminary note taking, work on an outline of your answer. This should not be a formal outline, but one that will be your roadmap to writing your answer. Note that this outline is solely for you. It does not count towards your grade. But preparing one is essential to writing your answer, which does count. Once you are satisfied with your outline, write your answer out in clear and neat handwriting and with careful presentation. If you have done your preparation in terms of keeping up with the material during the semester, studying before the exam, reading the question and outlining your answer, writing out the answer should entail expressing your response in a manner that someone else can understand and appreciate, i.e. grammatically correct English.

AN EXAMPLE

Here's what an outline to the practice exam question might look like:

1. S v. R

    Events in hotel lobby

Intentional torts

    Assault

    False imprisonment

    IIED

Negligent infliction of emotional distress

    Lack of physical impact

    Bystander liability–problem with relationship

Defamation

    Is accusatory tone of R's comments harmful to reputation?

        Reasonableness test

    Publication exists

    Damages: per quod versus per se issue

Confidential files

    Threshold problem of right defendant: discovery from other torts?

Misappropriation

    INS and Motorola: is this time sensitive?

    Trespass to chattels and conversion

Intrusion

Reasonable expectation of privacy: home versus business

2. R v. S

Web site

Threshold problem of right defendant: discovery if S brings suit?

Defamation

Defamatory statement: reasonableness standard

Per se and per quod

Publication to 3rd person: not an obstacle

Damages

Special damages: lost business? Causation problem potentially

Public disclosure of private facts

False Light

Right of publicity

Interference with contract or business advantage

Actual contracts?

Malice

Private detective

Intrusion

COMMENTS ON EXAMPLE OF ANSWER OUTLINE

There are several points to be gleaned from looking at the sample outline.

The purpose is to help you in organizing your thoughts and writing your answer. I will not look at it in grading your answer. Therefore, you should outline your answer in a way that is helpful to you rather than in a way that communicates to me that you know what you are doing. You do not need to write out the outline in detail, i.e. your answer outline need not lay out all the elements of the specific legal issues. But you should have that information laid out in your notes and class outline or keyed to your casebook for handy access.

The most important thing to notice is organization. The main organizational point is to follow the guidelines of the question. Note that you are asked two separate questions. The first question is about claims of Shelly against Ricky; the second, about claims of Ricky against Shelly. Keep them separate. Show the person reading your answer that you have at least the minimal intelligence to follow instructions. Note that each question is also organized around factual situations. That perhaps works the best for this question since you are presented with a complicated fact pattern. Within each factual scenario, the answer is broken down into relevant torts that are worth discussing. Not all torts are relevant to the factual scenarios presented. Focus on the ones that are the most salient.

The outline presents some special points to emphasize under each tort (such as special damages under defamation). Note that the outline does not provide much detail. That reflects the fact that I wrote the question and am familiar with what issues need to be emphasized and what the elements of the law are. You may want to put in more factual points based on the scenario in your outline. You should have the elements of law either well inculcated into your head or laid out in your course notes and outline. Keep in mind that you need to be prepared before you come into the exam. The preparation is based on having done the reading and preparing a comprehensive and useful set of course notes and outline based on your reading and classroom discussion. The more prepared you are before coming into the exam, the easier the experience will be in organizing your thoughts and writing your answer.

A SAMPLE ANSWER BASED ON THE OUTLINE

1.   Shelley v. Ricky

S. has several claims she can potentially raise against Ricky based first on the incident in the lobby and second on the office file.

Incident in lobby

S. can raise intentional tort claims, a negligence claim, and a defamation claim based on Ricky's conduct towards her in the lobby.

Intentional torts

S. can raise the claims of assault, false imprisonment, and intentional infliction of emotional distress (IIED). For each of these claims, S has to show that R. acted with intent. Under tort law, intent is shown either through improper or unlawful conduct or through knowledge with substantial certainty that harm would occur. The first means of showing intent, which is admittedly circular, can be established by R's abrasive conduct in a public place like the hotel lobby. Such conduct is inappropriate for the context. Intent can also be shown here with facts and circumstances indicating that R. knew how he was acting would be substantially certain to result in harm. Here, shouting at S and approaching her in an aggressive manner would support an argument that R had knowledge of what he was doing and that his actions were very likely to cause harm.

Intentional torts define a set of seven causes of action, each of which address a specific type of harm. The seven are battery, assault, false imprisonment, IIED, trespass to land, trespass to chattels, and conversion. Here, assault, false imprisonment, and IIED would be the most relevant.

Assault is an attempted battery. It addresses the apprehension felt by the plaintiff of an imminent battery. Here, R's aggressive conduct and his verbal abuse arguably made S. feel that she was about to be touched in an offensive or harmful manner (i.e. an imminent battery). R. may argue that he was fairly far from S when he said what he said and therefore not close enough for someone to be genuinely apprehensive. However, the facts do indicate that R did approach S and this might support S's claim of apprehension.

False imprisonment is an interference with the plaintiff's liberty to move. It can be physical, in terms of actual blockade of movement, or psychological, in terms of the plaintiff feeling trapped. S has an argument here that R's approach and his aggressive conduct restrained her freedom of movement. R has perhaps a stronger argument that S could have fled anytime and that she was not restrained at all. We would need some more facts about S's ability, both mentally and physically, to leave the situation under the circumstances.

IIED is perhaps the strongest of the three intentional tort claims. S needs to establish that R's conduct was extreme and outrageous and that it caused here emotional distress. Again, the circumstances and R's aggression would support such a claim. Furthermore, the fact that R pushed Lonny to the ground right in front of S. would also support an argument that R was acting in an extreme and outrageous manner. S would also have to establish that she suffered emotional distress that resulted from the outrageous conduct. Here, she may need psychiatric testimony or may need to point to some physical manifestation of her emotional distress or some other evidence supporting her claim of emotional injury. It is on this second prong of the tort that R. might have the most success in defending himself by showing that S has failed to provide sufficient evidence of injury to psyche.

Finally, there are traditionally several affirmative defenses to intentional torts, such as necessity, defense of self and property, consent, and insanity. None of these seem appropriate to the facts here. The success of S in raising these intentional tort claims may rest on her ability to make the prima facie case.

Negligence

A claim of negligence has four elements: duty, breach, causation, and damages. S's biggest problem in making a successful claim for negligence would stem from the last element, damages. R did not physically touch S and therefore there is no physical injury. S's only real avenue here is to raise a claim of bystander liability for the emotional distress of watching Lonny being hurt physically by R's negligent conduct. Courts typically look to three factors to determine whether recovery under bystander liability is available: (1) whether plaintiff was near the scene of the accident; (2) whether the plaintiff experienced sensory and contemporaneous observance of the accident; and (3) whether the plaintiff and the injured party were in a close relationship. The first two are relatively straightforward in this case since S was near Lonny when he was struck down and saw him be injured. The difficulty for S is her relationship with Lonny. Courts typically have found a close relationship based on a blood relationship (usually parent-child or sibling) or a marital relationship (husband-wife). Here, S and Lonny are described as intimate friends and that most likely will not be a relationship recognized under bystander liability. Perhaps, there are facts to support a case for common law marriage, but short of that, S's claim for negligence will most likely not be successful.

In addition to the relationship issue, S may have difficulties establishing a causal link between R's behavior and any emotional harm she suffers. She would also have problems establishing that R's conduct was unreasonable. The difficulty is that R's conduct seems to be better described as intentional rather than unreasonable, the former applying to purposive conduct, the latter to conduct that imposes a risk of harm on others. But these are not necessarily mutually exclusive and intentional conduct may also be unreasonable (although unreasonable conduct is not necessarily intentional). Courts may want to keep a bright line between intentional and unreasonable behavior so as not to have intentional torts be subsumed under negligence. If S finds herself in such a jurisdiction, she may have to choose between an intentional tort theory and a negligence theory as a basis for recovery of any emotional injury.

Defamation

R's request of S to "confess" made in a public case where third parties could hear is arguably defamatory. To make a case for defamation, S has to establish that R made a defamatory statement, published it to the third parties, and that the publication resulted in damages (which will be presumed for per se defamation and libel). The key question here is whether the statement is defamatory, which means that the statement is reasonably likely to cause harm to the plaintiff's reputation in the community. R's statement does not appear to be defamatory on its face, but the implication is that S has done something wrong that she should confess. The implication is arguably quite tenuous here and S would have to bring in extrinsic evidence to show that people would understand what R was implying. Establishing that people would understand R's implication may be difficult since it is not clear whether everyone knew about the defaced web site. Even if it could be established that people would understand the implication, it is not clear that the implication that S defaced a web site or defamed R thereby is itself defamatory. A reasonable person might find such conduct childish or perhaps aggressive, but not criminal or indicative of bad, unprofessional behavior. Most likely, S will not be able to establish the defamatory nature of R's statement to her.

If she could, perhaps it would fall into the per se category of criminal or unlawful conduct. If so, damages are presumed. If the statement is defamatory but not per se, then the statement is defamatory per quod, meaning that S would have to show special damages, such as harm to her business, that resulted from R's statement. It is not clear what damages would be here since we do not have enough facts. Even if S could establish these damages, R may have the defense of truth (that S actually did do what he implied), privilege (very tenuous here since R told a whole group of people who may have been largely strangers) and the First Amendment. For the privilege defense, R would have to establish that he was protecting some mutual interest with the persons to whom he made he statement. Since he told a large group, most likely the privilege would be lost. For the First Amendment defense, R would have to establish that S is a public figure, which is possible if she had some degree of celebrity or notoriety in Sprawl. If R can establish S as a public figure, then S would have to also establish that R acted with knowledge of the falsity of his statement or reckless disregard to its truth. Under these facts, S may be able to establish reckless disregard, since at the time R was only speculating as to who defaced the web site and did not investigate or have any real factual basis to blame S for the misdeed.

Confidential Files

There is a threshold problem of bringing claims against R for the alleged appropriation of the confidential files since S does not know that R in fact did look at the files or in fact ask Tony to infiltrate her office. This analysis assumes that S can establish that R had something to do with the files. Perhaps S can uncover information in the course of discovery for the much more solid claims discussed above to bolster her case regarding the files.

Misappropriation

Misappropriation results from a party appropriating the fruits of the effort of a competitor. The tort originated in the famous INS case which involved the misappropriation of news. The INS case, post-Erie, is not longer precedential although some courts have adopted its principles. The Second Circuit, in *NBA v. Motorola*, laid out the following five elements to the claim of misappropriation: 1. plaintiff gathered information at a cost; 2. Information is time sensitive; 3. Defendant's use constitutes free riding of plaintiff's effort; 4. plaintiff and defendant are direct competitors; and 5.

Defendant's free riding would substantially reduce the incentive of plaintiff to gather the information.

If S raised a misappropriation claim against R for taking the information in the files, she should readily be able to establish the fourth element, but would have problems with the other four. The big problem is that S's client, not S, gathered the information. Therefore, elements 1, 3, and 5 would be difficult to show. Furthermore, it would be difficult to argue that the information was time sensitive. Unlike the sports scores or the news, the information about a real estate development plan would be valuable for a long, rather than a short period of time. For these reasons, the misappropriation claim may not be successful.

Trespass to chattel/Conversion

These two intentional torts protect possessory and ownership interests in personal property. If in fact the files were taken and copied, for example, there is arguably some sort of interference with S's possessory or ownership interest in the files and the information contained therein. The difficulty posed by these claims is identifying the personal property. The files are of course personal property, but they were not damaged in any way and therefore it may be impossible to raise a claim based on an invasion of an interest in the files. The key question is whether the information in the files is personal property. If they are personal property, and the information had been copied, there is arguably an interference with possessory and ownership interest in the information. So, is the information in the files property? On the one hand, information is different from tangible forms of property, such as land or chattels. Since information can be copied readily and disseminated widely, it lacks the usual exclusivity that we may associate with property. On the other hand, information is valuable and therefore treatment of information as property may be necessary to legally protect important economic interests.

With respect to the files, the concern with blurring the distinction between person and things is not relevant. Furthermore, there is no equivalent concern with giving S a windfall. In fact, there is a case for not allowing R to obtain a windfall from sneaking a peak at the information. Therefore, property treatment may be appropriate. However, there may be other means to protect S's interests here, such as the intrusion claim discussed below.

Finally, if the trespass/conversion claim is allowed S would still have the difficulty of establishing compensatory damages for recovery. It is not clear how the information has been damaged by the taking. Perhaps the project is less valuable because of the new competition for the purchase of land around the planned site. But arguably the information itself has not been destroyed or damaged and consequently S may not be able to recover under these claims.

Intrusion

S also has a claim against R for intrusion. This privacy based claim entails interference with S's reasonable expectation of privacy by R's conduct. S's argument is that R invaded a place which S reasonably expected to be private when R hired Tony to go through S's files and take the file containing the confidential plans. R would argue that S does not have a reasonable expectation of privacy in her place of business. However, R does not seem to have legitimate interest, such as uncovering fraud, to intrude. Most likely, S has a fairly strong claim here.

2.   R v. S

R has potential claims based on (1) the defacing of the web page and (2) the use of the private detective to follow him around. The threshold problem that R has for each of these claims is showing that S is the correct defendant. After all, R has no real idea who did the things to the web page and he may not even be aware of the private detective. But some of this information may be discoverable in a suit the S brings against R for the claims discussed in question one. Otherwise, R may have to do some independent investigation in order to connect S to the activities discussed below. The analysis proceeds under the assumption that R can establish S's activities, rebutting any SODDI defense by S.

Web Page

The key claims arising from these facts are defamation, public disclosure of private facts, false light, right of publicity, intentional infliction of emotional distress, and interference with contract or prospective business advantage.

Defamation

I refer the reader to my discussion of the elements of a defamation claim presented above in question one. Here, R will have little trouble showing that the statements are defamatory and defamatory per se. These statements allege R's adultery and professional integrity through statements about cheating, lying, and stealing other people's property. Since the statements were made in a web page on a presumably publicly available site, R can establish the second element of publication to a third party. Finally, R's damages would be presumed either because these statements are defamatory per se or because they constitute libel, or recorded defamation.

S would raise the defense of truth and First Amendment. Privilege would most likely not apply since the publication was essentially to the whole world by placement on the Internet and not targeted to a group who may have a shared interest in knowing about the information. S's First Amendment defense would rest on R's status as a public figure, which may be particularly strong here given all the advertisements containing R's image. The First Amendment defense would require R to show that S acted with knowledge of falsity or with reckless disregard. The first may be difficult since S had some belief that what she was saying was true. Reckless disregard also may be difficult to establish since S did hire an investigator to collect data that could back up most of the assertions.

Public Disclosure of Private Facts

This tort addresses disclosures of a person's private affairs, which are truthful, but offensive to a person of ordinary sensibilities. R has a claim against S for the disclosure about his car being parked at a hotel as disclosure of a private fact. S would not have a First Amendment defense here under *Cox* because she is not a member of the media.

False Light

Some jurisdictions treat a false light claim like a defamation claim. If the two claims are not merged, R has to show that the information on the doctored web site presents a false representation of him. R has the burden under the claim of false light to show the falsity of the statements on the web site. S would have a First Amendment defense requiring R to show actual malice on the part of S; the analysis of actual malice would be similar to the discussion of defamation above.

Right of publicity

Since the doctored web site uses elements associated with R's public persona (such as the Volvo), there is a possible claim that S has appropriated R's publicity for a commercial purpose, as in Vanna White. S has a defense that there was no commercial purpose for the appropriation and the purpose was to publicize or comment on R's activities. R could show a commercial purpose by pointing to S using the doctored web site to steal away R's customers. Finally, S may have a First Amendment defense despite *Zacchini* since she did not appropriate the full value of R's publicity. However, *Zacchini* does not clarify what such a First Amendment defense would look like.

IIED

R also has a claim that S's doctoring of the web site was extreme and outrageous conduct that resulted in his emotional distress. The problems with causation discussed above in question one would apply here as well.

Intentional Interference with Contact or Prospective Business Advantage

R has a claim that the doctoring of the web site was a malicious act that caused parties to breach an existing contract or caused parties to break off business dealings with R. R would have to show that actual contracts had been broken as a result of the doctored web site or that parties decided not to deal with R because of the doctored we site to establish these claims.

Private Detective

The main claim that R could raise is one of intrusion if the detective engaged in conduct that interfered with R's reasonable expectation of privacy. It appears that the detective simply followed R around in a public place, but did not invade his home or other private space. Therefore, this claim may be difficult to raise. Notice that this claim would be against S even though it is the detective that is allegedly intrusive since the detective was hired by S.

COMMENTS ON SAMPLE ANSWER

This sample answer is provided as a guide for the type of analysis and writing that will be expected on the final exam. This essay is not intended to be a perfect answer although it does a good job of hitting all the major issues and a good job of analyzing and applying the law. More use of the facts could have been made particularly in discussing some of the privacy torts and interference with contract/prospective advantage. But if you study the question and answer carefully, you should get a sense of the type of analysis that will be expected.

Notice that there is very little use of case names. In general, the answer makes careful use of legal doctrines and principles with occasional reference to cases. In citing cases, two mistakes to avoid are misstating the legal and principle to be applied and to simply recite a case name without adequate discussion of what the case means and how it is to be applied.

Notice that the answer discusses all pertinent legal issues even those that are not likely to be successful or are substantially deficient. Do not prejudge your answer. The point of your response is to present and assess as thoroughly as possible all potential claims that the facts could give rise to.

Finally, notice the presentation and organization of the answer. Not only is it generally well written, the answer contains headings and flags that signal to the reader the structure of the response and the flow of the argument.

Exam Checklists

I. Overview

A. Keep in mind the three big questions:

    1. Standard of Care: intent, negligence, or strict liability.

        a. These three are not mutually exclusive. You should consider how each apply to the same fact pattern.

    2. Cause of action: what is the tort cause of action that the plaintiff must prove in order to obtain a remedy from the defendant.

        a. Intentional tort: seven distinct causes of action might apply—battery, assault, false imprisonment, trespass to land, trespass to chattel, conversion, and intentional infliction of emotional distress.

        b. Negligence: plaintiff must show duty, breach, causation, and compensable damages.

        c. Strict liability: arises in three distinct situations:

            (i) Dangerous animals.

            (ii) Ultra-hazardous activities.

            (iii) Strict products liability.

B.   Tort Policy

    1.   Compensation of injured party.

    2.   Deterrence of party from conduct that causes injury.

    3.   Law and economics:

       a.   Internalization of costs.

       b.   Avoid deterrence of beneficial conduct.

       c.   Coase Theorem: parties will negotiate to recover harm and therefore if transaction costs are low, tort law is irrelevant. However, if transaction costs are high, then tort law should try to impose liability and damages the way the parties would if they could negotiate.

    4.   Criticism of Law and Economics:

       a.   Fairness, not efficiency, is goal of Tort law.

       b.   Tort law should try to pursue justice by compensating victims who are underprivileged or otherwise underrepresented because of race or gender.

II.   Intentional Torts: Prima Facie Case and Defenses

A.   Keep in mind three issues in analyzing intentional torts:

    1.   The defendant must have acted with intent

    2.   The defendant's act must fall within one or more of the seven intentional torts.

    3.   The defendant may have a defense which would make the defendant not liable for the tort.

B.   Intent:

    1.   General standard: to show that defendant acted with intent, plaintiff must show either:

       a.   defendant acted with the purpose of producing the consequence of the act; or

b.   defendant acted with the knowledge that the consequence of the act would occur with substantial certainty.

2.   Special issue: dual intent. The general view is that the
defendant intended the act, not the consequences of the act.
However, some jurisdictions require dual intent: the defendant
must have intended both the act and the harm that was the
consequence of the act.

C.   The Seven Intentional Torts: Remember the elements and
issues raised for each claim:

1.   Battery: defendant intended to cause a harmful or offensive contact with the physical person of another and such contact
either directly or indirectly occurred.

a.   Most jurisdictions require only that the defendant
intended the contact not that the contact be harmful or
offensive. However, in dual intent jurisdictions, the defendant
must intend that there is contact and that the contact is
harmful or offensive.

b.   Harm occurs if there is physical injury, even a
relatively minor one.

c.   Offense occurs if the contact offends a reasonable
sense of dignity.

2.   Assault: defendant intended either (a) to cause a harmful
or offensive contact with the person of another or (b) to cause
immediate apprehension of a harmful or offensive contact and the
plaintiff thereby is put in immediate apprehension of a harmful or
offensive contact.

a.   If a defendant's conduct results in a harmful or
offensive contact, the defendant is liable for battery only. An
assault claim merges into a battery claim if a harmful or
offensive contact occurs. If there is only an immediate apprehension of a harmful or offensive contact, but no actual
contact, then the defendant is liable for an assault, not a
battery.

b. The apprehension by the plaintiff must be imminent. A conditional threat of future harm cannot be the basis for an assault claim.

3.   False Imprisonment: defendant (1) intentionally confines a plaintiff, (2) against the plaintiff's will, and (3) the plaintiff is aware of the confinement.

a.   Plaintiff must be completely confined with no reasonable means of escape. If the means of escape imposes a risk of harm to a plaintiff, the plaintiff's personal property, or to third parties, then confinement is complete.

4.   Intentional infliction of emotional distress: defendant intentionally caused severe emotional distress in plaintiff by engaging in extreme and outrageous conduct.

a.   Extreme and outrageous conduct is determined by community standards, usually based on the average member of the community.

5.   Trespass to land: defendant (a) intentionally enters, or causes a thing or a third party to enter, the land in possession of another, (b) intentionally remains on the land after permission to be on the land is removed, or (c) intentionally fails to remove from the land an item that the defendant is obligated to remove.

a.   Plaintiff does not have to show any harm to the land or to the person to recover for trespass to land. The injury is in the violation of the plaintiff's right to exclusive possession of the land.

6.   Trespass to chattels: defendant (a) intentionally dispossessed another person of personal property or (b) intentionally used or intermeddled through physical contact with the personal property in possession of another.

a.   Unlike trespass to land, trespass to chattels requires the plaintiff to show actual harm that resulted from the trespass to personal property. This actual harm can include loss of use for a significant period of time, harm to the plaintiff's person or personal property, or damage to the condition of the personal property.

7. Conversion: defendant intentionally exercised dominion or control over the personal property of plaintiff so as to seriously interfere with the right of the plaintiff to control the personal property.

    a. A plaintiff need not show actual harm to recover under conversion.

    b. Conversion and trespass to chattels both cover intentional torts against personal property. Conversion covers interference with the plaintiff's rights of ownership and control over the personal property. Trespass to chattels covers interference with a plaintiff's rights of possession over the personal property.

D. Defenses: a defendant can raise several defenses against plaintiff's claim of an intentional tort. These defenses apply to all the intentional torts. Remember that a defendant has the burden to raise and prove these defenses.

1. Consent: plaintiff agreed to defendant's conduct that resulted in the intentional tort. The agreement can be express (such as through a contract) or implied through the conduct of the plaintiff.

    a. Consent has boundaries, and if a defendant's conduct goes beyond these boundaries, then consent does not apply. The scope of consent depends on the facts and circumstances of the case and the standards of society for the behavior at issue.

    b. A plaintiff's consent must be informed. If consent is obtained by trickery or force, then the defense does not apply. The amount of information necessary is based on what a reasonable person would need to know in order to agree to defendant's conduct.

    c. A defendant can raise defense of consent if a reasonable person would have believed that the plaintiff had consented and the defendant in fact did believe that the plaintiff had consented.

2.   Defense of self: defendant can use reasonable force if the defendant reasonably believes that a plaintiff is about to commit harmful conduct on the defendant. The threatened conduct can be any type of tort, intentional, negligent, or strict liability.

    a.   For force to be reasonable, it must not be disproportionate to the threatened harm. Deadly force is reasonable only if the threat reasonably appears to be deadly or of serious bodily harm.

    b.   Courts are split on whether a defendant is required to retreat. Some jurisdictions hold that self-defense is not available if a defendant could reasonably have retreated from the threatened harm. Other jurisdictions do not require retreat.

3.   Defense of third parties: as with self-defense, defendant can use reasonable use to protect a third party who reasonable appears to be in imminent harm. Some jurisdictions require that the third party must have actually been subjected to imminent harm.

4.   Defense of property: defendant can use reasonable force to prevent intrusion or dispossession of property. Before using reasonable force, a defendant must first ask a party to cease and desist from the interference with property. A defendant can never use deadly force in defense of property.

    a.   In the case of personal property, defendant can take reasonable steps to recapture the personal property only if the defendant acts timely after the dispossession with the personal property or after his discovery of the dispossession.

5.   Defense of private necessity: defendant has the right to interfere with a plaintiff's property in order to mitigate or avoid an imminent private harm or injury arising from a natural occurrence or some event unrelated to the plaintiff's use of the property.

a.   A defendant will have to pay a plaintiff reasonable compensation for any harm that occurs to plaintiff's property from the defendant's interference.

6.   Defense of public necessity: defendant, usually the state or a public official, has the right to interfere with plaintiff's property in order to avoid an imminent social injury.

b.   A defendant does not have to pay a plaintiff compensation for the harm to the property from defendant's interference.

E.   Remedies: if a defendant is found liable for an intentional tort, the defendant must compensate a plaintiff for the injury and may be liable for punitive damages. See Chapter Eight for more details.

F.   Nuisance: consists of two separate legal claims, a private nuisance or a public nuisance.

1.   Private nuisance: an invasion of a private use and enjoyment of land that is

a.   EITHER intentional and unreasonable, where an invasion is unreasonable if

(i)   the gravity of the harm outweighs the benefit of the defendant's conduct, or

(ii)   the harm caused by the conduct is serious and the financial burden of compensating for the harm would not make the defendant's activities feasible;

b.   OR unintentional and arising out of negligent or reckless conduct or abnormally dangerous conditions or activities.

2.   Public nuisance: unreasonable interference with a right common to the general public. An interference is unreasonable if it has a significant effect on public safety, peace, health, comfort or convenience or if the activity has a significant effect on a public right, that may be defined by statute.

III.   Negligence: Duty of Care

A.   Elements of Negligence Claim: A plaintiff must establish duty, breach, causation, and damages. Keep these four elements in mind as you work through Chapters Three through Six.

B.   The Duty of Care element: General duty

1.   Under negligence, there is a general duty to act in a reasonable manner. From this perspective, duty is an easy element to establish—but keep in mind the special cases that are laid out below.

2.   The duty element is a question of law, which means that a judge ultimately determines whether a defendant owed a duty to a plaintiff. The duty question does not depend on factual issues to be determined by a jury.

C.   Special Duty Issues

1.   Nonfeasance or Omission: A defendant does not have a duty to rescue another person. In general, failure to rescue someone does not give rise to liability under negligence or Tort law more generally.

a.   Exception to no duty to rescue rule: If a defendant undertook a course of conduct that placed a plaintiff in danger, then the defendant owes the plaintiff a duty of care to rescue the plaintiff. Remember: "danger invites rescue."

2.   Special relationship: If a defendant is in a special relationship with a plaintiff, then is the defendant has a duty to act.

a.   Custodial relationship is an example of a special relationship: Suppose a defendant has been hired to take care of a plaintiff, such as a bodyguard or caregiver. Under these custodial situations, the defendant owes the plaintiff a duty of care to take reasonable steps to protect the plaintiff. Note that this relationship may be voluntary on the part of the defendant or imposed by law on the defendant (such as through a guardianship).

b.   Landowners owe special duties to those who come onto the land and are injured. Some jurisdictions have created a general duty of care that a landowner owes to anyone who comes lawfully onto the land. Most jurisdictions define the duty based on the reason the person came onto the land.

   (i) Duty to trespassers: No duty is owed to a trespasser except not to intentionally injure the trespasser.

   (ii) Duty to invitee: A general duty of care is owed to an invitee—someone who comes onto the land by invitation of a landowner for the landowner's business.

   (iii) Duty to licensee: A duty to warn of known defects and keep the property reasonably safe of known hazards is owed to a licensee, who is someone who comes onto the land with the limited permission of a landowner for some purpose other than the landowner's business.

   c.   If a defendant has control over a third party, then there is a duty to take care that the third party does not harm other parties. An example of this situation would be a parent's obligation to control a child or an employer's obligation to control an employee in the workplace.

   (i) *Tarasoff* duties: A psychiatrist has a duty towards a foreseeable plaintiff who may be harmed by the psychiatrist's patient.

   3.   Public Policy: There can be limits on the duty of care owed by public utilities and governmental entities to individual plaintiffs. In general, there is no duty of care owed to a particular plaintiff by a public utility or a governmental entity if the entity does not take reasonable steps to protect the public. Legal liability in these situations is limited to obligations owed under contract and to intentional tort claims.

   4.   Emotional harm: In general, a defendant does not owe a duty for emotional harm that a bystander suffers when he witnesses a tort committed by the defendant. The exception is if a bystander is in the zone of danger created by a defendant's conduct and witnesses a close relative injured by the defendant. To be in the "zone of danger," the bystander must have almost been physically injured by the defendant. A close relative includes a parent, a sibling, or an offspring.

5. Economic harm: In general, a defendant does not owe a duty for economic harm suffered by a plaintiff unless the economic harm comes from a physical impact to the plaintiff's property or person. An exception to this rule is the duty owed by an accountant or attorney for professional malpractice that arises from professional malpractice.

III. Negligence: Breach through Unreasonable Conduct

A. A plaintiff establishes breach of duty by showing that a defendant's conduct was unreasonable. The standard of reasonableness is meant to be a flexible one that depends on the particular facts of a case and the case's context. The reason the standard is flexible is to allow the law to evolve to reflect changing attitudes, and to allow people to act and conform their conduct to the standard. The major criticism of the reasonableness standard is lack of predictability and notice.

B. Whether a defendant's conduct is unreasonable is a matter for a jury to decide, although in some instances, when violation of the standard is clear and the courts have had experience with a particular set of facts, the question of reasonableness is a question for a judge, who can take the question away from the jury.

C. There are five types of arguments that are commonly used to establish the reasonableness of a defendant's conduct. Whenever you are faced with an issue of breach, or the reasonableness of a defendant's conduct, you should work through this list to develop arguments on the side of the plaintiff and the defendant.

1. Custom: The way people usually behave in a particular situation, also known as custom, can be evidence of what is reasonable. Failure to act according to custom can be evidence of acting unreasonably while compliance with custom can be evidence of acting reasonably. Custom, however, is never conclusive evidence of reasonableness except in a medical malpractice case. Evidence of custom provides some basis for determining reasonableness. There is always a question, however, of whether the custom itself is reasonable.

a. Industry standard is evidence of custom. Non-compliance with industry standards can be evidence of unreasonableness and compliance, evidence of reasonableness. But as with all custom-based evidence, an industry standard is not conclusive.

2.   The Hand Formula: The balance of costs and benefits can be evidence of reasonableness. The balancing of costs and benefits is associated with Judge Learned Hand and is often also referred to as the BpL analysis, or BpL test. The B refers to the burden or cost of a particular conduct. The p is the probably of harm that can arise from not following a particular course of conduct and L is the extent of harm that can arise from not following a particular course of conduct. According to the Hand Formula, if B is greater than the p times L (BpL), then not doing the conduct is reasonable. If B is less than p times L (B

3.   Statutes: A violation of a statute can be the basis to establish the unreasonableness of a defendant's conduct if (i) the harm a plaintiff suffered is a type of harm the statute was meant to prevent; (ii) the plaintiff is in a class of persons the statute was meant to protect; and (iii) the statute establishes a standard of conduct. If the statute meets these three criteria, then violation of the statute is negligence per se. In a few jurisdictions, violation of the statute is treated as evidence of unreasonableness, rather than negligence per se.

4.   *Res ipsa loquitur*: Sometimes the fact that an accident happened is evidence of unreasonableness—in other words, "the act speaks for itself." *Res ipsa loquitur* applies when (i) an accident occurred as a result of an instrumentality that was in control of a defendant; (ii) the accident is of a type that would not have occurred unless someone had acted unreasonably; and (iii) a plaintiff did not contribute to the accident.

5.   Special categories of reasonable people: In general, reasonableness is an objective standard that doesn't consider the special characteristics of a particular defendant. There are two exceptions to this general proposition.

(a) Children: When a child is being held liable for a

non-adult activity, then the age, intelligence, and experience of the child are taken into consideration. If a child, however, is involved in an adult activity, the child's characteristics are not considered and the child's conduct is judged by an objective standard of reasonableness.

(b) Physical condition: If a defendant has a physical condition, such as loss of sight or loss of a limb, then the physical condition is accounted for in determining the reasonableness of the defendant's conduct. This rule does not apply to any mental conditions of a defendant.

V. Negligence: Factual and Legal Causation

A.   Causation: plaintiff must show that the defendant's unreasonable conduct caused the injury suffered by the plaintiff. Causation requires showing a connection, or nexus, between the defendant's unreasonable act and the injury. There are two parts to causation: factual causation and legal causation.

B.   Factual causation: requires the plaintiff to show that there is a factual connection between the unreasonable conduct and the injury. Courts have devised tests for factual causation based upon the number of causes at issue in a case.

1.   Single cause: if there is only one cause for the injury, then courts apply the but for test for factual causation. Under the but for test, plaintiff must show that but for the defendant's unreasonable conduct, the injury would not have occurred.

2.   Multiple causes: if there are possibly more than one cause for the injury, then courts apply the substantial factor test for factual causation. Under the substantial factor test, plaintiff must show that the defendant's unreasonable act was more likely thank other factors to have caused the plaintiff's injury.

a.   Special case of *Summers v. Tice*: when there are multiple defendants and each are equally likely to have caused the accident, then the burden shifts to each defendant to show that they were not the substantial factor. Absent this special rule, all the defendants could be found to be not liable even though one of them must have caused the injury. A special application of the *Summers v. Tice* rule is market share liability: when a product caused a harm but the plaintiff cannot show which manufacturer produced the specific product that the plaintiff used, then each manufacturer will be held liable for the damages based on market share. Under the market share liability rule, each manufacturer will have the burden to show it did not produce the product that caused the harm. If a manufacturer cannot prove they did not cause it, then the market share rule applies.

3.   Factual Causation and Uncertainty: in some cases, there might be scientific uncertainty as to the cause of the plaintiff's injury. Environmental or other factors might have contributed to the plaintiff's injury. In such cases, expert testimony is often used to establish factual connection, and the causation element might boil down to a battle of the experts.

C.   Legal causation: also know as proximate causation, this part of causation requires the plaintiff to show that the injury is not the remote consequences of defendant's unreasonable conduct. Courts use two tests to analyze legal causation: the directness test and the foreseeability test.

1.   Directness test: if the injury can be directly connected to the unreasonable conduct without an unforeseeable, intervening cause, then the unreasonable conduct is the legal cause of the injury. An unforeseeable, intervening cause is called superseding because it cuts off liability for the defendant.

2.   Foreseeability test: if the injury is the foreseeable consequence of the unreasonable conduct, then the unreasonable conduct is the legal cause of the injury. The foreseeability test cuts off liability for injury that is not the predictable consequence of the unreasonable conduct. An important exception to the foreseeability test is the egg shell plaintiff rule: the defendant is liable for all personal injuries that are the direct and factual result of the unreasonable conduct even if the injury was not foreseeable. In other words, the defendant "is liable for the plaintiff as he finds him."

3.   Legal policy: causation tends to be the most difficult part of the negligence claim. Courts sometimes become confused themselves. The best way to keep these issues clear is to work through the factual and legal causation parts systematically and run each causation issue through these various tests. Keep in mind, however, the overriding policy concern with holding a defendant liable for risky situations that are created by the defendant's unreasonable conduct.

VI.   Negligence: Recoverable Damages

A.   Damages is the fourth element of claim for negligence. A plaintiff must show that a defendant's unreasonable conduct resulted in damages.

B.   Survival and wrongful death actions are mechanisms that allow the estate or a surviving relative of a tort victim to bring claims after the tort victim has died.

C.   Categories of recoverable damages include pecuniary and non-pecuniary damages. Pecuniary damages are monetary injuries, such as medical bills, property damage, and lost wages. Non-pecuniary damages are pain and suffering, loss of enjoyment of life, and loss of consortium.

VII.   Strict Liability

A.   Strict liability is the third standard of care for tort liability. Strict liability imposes liability for harm caused by a defendant regardless of intent or unreasonable conduct.

B.   To establish a claim for strict liability, a plaintiff has to establish duty, breach, causation and damages.

1.   For strict liability claims, duty arises in three instances:

(a) duty to prevent harm from wild animals one owns or possesses;

(b) duty to prevent harm from abnormally dangerous activities;

(c) duty to prevent harm from defective products.

2. The breach element of strict liability does not require the plaintiff to establish that the defendant acted unreasonably. For strict liability, breach requires the plaintiff to establish that the defendant failed to carry out one of the three duties defendant had under strict liability.

3. The elements of causation and damages under strict liability are similar to those under negligence.

C. Special rules to remember about strict liability:

1. Strict liability for wild animals may also apply to domestic animals with known dangerous tendencies.

2. Courts use a multifactor test in determining whether an activity is abnormally dangerous.

3. The duty to prevent harm from defective products applies to manufacturers, distributors, and sellers of the product.

VIII. Tort Remedies

A. After a plaintiff has established a tort claim against a defendant, the court will award the plaintiff a remedy for the injuries suffered. Although a plaintiff might have multiple claims for the same injury, there can be only one remedy for the injury suffered.

B. Injunctions are one type of remedy. They are a court order telling the defendant to do something or to refrain from doing something. Injunctions are often used as a remedy for trespass to land and for more advanced tort claims based on products liability, defamation, or business torts.

C. Damages are another type of remedy and the preferred type in most tort cases. Damages are an award of money to the plaintiff as a remedy for a tort claim. There are two types: compensatory and punitive.

1. Compensatory damages are an amount of money calculated to compensate the plaintiff for the injury suffered. The plaintiff must prove the amount of compensatory damages. Some states have imposed caps on the non-pecuniary aspect of compensatory damages.

a.   Plaintiff has a duty to mitigate damages.

b.   A judge has discretion to award prejudgment interest.

c.   A judge will discount damages for future losses.

d.   The collateral source rule states that compensatory damages will not be reduced by the amount of compensation that the plaintiff has received from other sources, such as insurance.

2.   Punitive damages are an amount of money calculated to punish the defendant for malicious or grossly reckless conduct.

a.   Punitive damages cannot be grossly excessive or they violate the Due Process Clause of the U.S. Constitution.

(i) Grossly excessive is determined by considering (a) the reprehensibility of the conduct, (b) the ratio of punitive to compensatory damages, and (c) the comparison to sanctions for similar conduct under criminal or other law.

(ii) In general, single digit ratios of punitive to compensatory damages are not grossly excessive.

(iii) Reprehensibility is determined by (a) physical injury, (b) indifference or disregard of defendant, (c) repeated action by defendant, and (d) intent or malice of defendant.

(iv) Injuries to parties not represented in the litigation cannot be a basis to determine the amount of punitive damages.

b.   States have enacted various limitations of punitive damages. Such limitations include:

(i) Bifurcated trials.

(ii) Decoupling of punitive and compensatory damages.

(iii) Enumeration of factors for determining punitive damages.

(iv) Caps on punitive damages expressed as multiples of pecuniary damages.

IX. Defenses to Negligence and Strict Liability

A.   There are two types of defenses to negligence and strict liability claims: defenses based on the conduct of the plaintiff and defenses based on the status of the defendant.

B.   Defenses based on the conduct of the plaintiff.

1.   Assumption of risk: a defense based on voluntary and knowing undertaking of a risky activity.

a.   Express assumption of risk: based on contract, specifically an exculpatory clause. Enforcement of the contract term is based on the Tunkl factors:

(i) the defendant is in a business that is thought suitable for public regulation;

(ii) the defendant is performing a service of great importance to the public, which is often a matter of practical necessity for some members of the public;

(iii) the defendant holds himself out as willing to perform the service for any member of the public who seeks it;

(iv) because of the necessity of the service provided, the defendant has a bargaining advantage against members of the public who seek the service;

(v) the defendant seeks exculpation through a standard adhesion contract and does not provide the option of obtaining protection against injury by paying additional fees;

(vi) the defendant in rendering service obtains control over the person or property of the person obtaining the service.

b.   Primary assumption of risk: applies to inherent and known risks of an activity when carried out according to the rules of the game;

c.   Secondary, or implied assumption of risk: applies to plaintiff's voluntary and knowing undertaking of an activity outside of an express contract.

2.   Contributory negligence: applies to plaintiff's unreasonable conduct that caused plaintiff's injury.

a.   Applies only to negligence claims.

b.   Completely bars recovery by the plaintiff.

c.   Last clear chance doctrine allows the plaintiff to rebut the defense if the plaintiff can show that the defendant had the chance to avoid the accident.

3.   Comparative negligence: requires the court to compare the relative fault of the parties and express the relative contribution of the parties to the injuries in percentage terms.

a.   Percentages are used to allocate the damages to the plaintiff. Under a pure system, plaintiff recovers the percentage of damages that are attributed to the defendants. Under a modified system, plaintiff recovers the percentage of damages only if the defendants have a greater percentage than the plaintiff.

b.   Only four states and the District of Columbia retain contributory negligence.

c.   States vary in how assumption of risk is treated under comparative negligence.

(i) All states retain express assumption of risk as a complete defense.

(ii) Some states subsume secondary assumption of risk under comparative negligence while retaining primary assumption of risk as a separate defense.

(iii) Other states subsume both primary and secondary assumption of risk under comparative negligence.

C.   Defenses based on the status of the defendant.

1.   Charitable immunity: all states have abrogated with some retaining immunity from negligence for volunteers in charitable entities.

2.   Interfamily immunity: most states have abrogated spousal immunity and some states have abrogated parental immunity.

3.   Sovereign immunity: abrogation through statute at the federal and state levels.

X.   Multiple Defendants

A.   Joint and several liability: allows a plaintiff to obtain the judgment for the full amount of damages against one of many defendants.

1.   It should be distinguished from joint liability and several liability.

2.   It arises in one of three situations:

a.   Concerted action.

b.   Joint duty.

c.   Indivisible harm.

3.   The defendant found liable under joint and several liability can obtain a judgment against the other defendants for the proportionate share under a claim for indemnity or for contribution.

B.   Vicarious liability: imputes liability to a party based on the tortious conduct of someone over whom the party has responsibility or control.

1.   Under vicarious liability, a party can be liable even though they did not commit a tort.

2.   The party can also be held liable under joint and several liability.

3.   The party can also be held liable under a negligent supervision or a negligent entrustment claim.

4.   Vicarious liability arises in four situations:

a.   Liability of an employer for the torts committed by an employee in the scope of employment.

b.   Liability of a hiring party for the activity of an independent contractor involving a nondelegable duty.

c.   In some jurisdictions, liability of a parent for the intentional or malicious acts of a child.

d.   In some jurisdictions, liability of the owner of an automobile for the tortious acts of a driver.

C.   Special Issues Under Comparative Negligence.

1.   A plaintiff can settle with one defendant and continue litigation with the remaining defendants.

a.   The amount of settlement will be offset against the final judgment either on a dollar-per-dollar amount or on the proportionate share of the settling defendant's liability.

b.   Non-settling defendants cannot seek contribution from a settling defendant.

c.   A settling defendant can seek contribution from non-settling defendants if the amount of settlement is greater than the proportionate share of liability and the settling defendant received a release from the non-settling ones.

2.   Imputed contributory negligence imputes the negligence of a third party to the plaintiff. Jurisdictions that adopt the doctrine impute contributory negligence only if negligence is imputed.

3.   Many jurisdictions grapple with the issue of how to handle claims of intentional torts against some defendants and negligence against others. Some jurisdictions treat all tort claims

under a proportionate fault approach. Others have adopted statutes to treat intentional tort claims differently for the purposes of apportionment.

XI. Products Liability

A.   The law of products liability constitutes three tort based claims: negligence, strict products liability, and misrepresentation.

B.   Negligence claims have the four traditional elements: duty, breach, causation, and damages.

 1.   Privity of contract was a limitation on duty in negligence claims for defective products. The famous case of MacPherson did away with the privity requirement and imposed a duty not to sell a product negligently made regardless of lack of contract.

 2.   Unreasonable conduct is established by showing that the defendant engaged in conduct that fell below the standard of care, using the methods of showing breach discussed in Chapter Four.

C.   Strict products liability claims hold the seller of a defective product liable for physical harm to purchasers or users and their product without regard to fault on the part of the seller.

 1.   Strict product liability has its roots in the law of warranties and in the application of strict liability to ultrahazardous activities.

 2.   The key issue in a strict products liability case is whether a product is defective. There are three types of defects.

  a.   Manufacturing defect: the product was made incorrectly in the factory. This type of defect is shown by the product not functioning as expected.

  b.   Design defect: the product was designed in an improper way. This is shown through either the consumer expectations test or the risk-utility test.

  c.   Warning defect: the seller failed to warn about dangers that they knew or should have known about. The warning must be informative to a reasonable consumer to be adequate.

3.   A product whose inherent characteristics are dangerous is not defective.

D.   Misrepresentation is another claim that is brought as part of a products liability cause of action. The elements of misrepresentation are presented in Chapter Thirteen.

E.   Special defenses in products liability cases: the defenses for negligence and strict liability claims discussed in Chapter Nine apply to products liability. In addition, there are special defenses to also keep in mind.

1.   Not a product: strict product liability claims do not apply to the sale of services or of land.

2.   State of the art: for design defect claims, the defendant can point to the state of technology at the time a product was made to defend against a claim of defective design. Some jurisdictions reject this defense on the ground that sellers of products need to keep up with developments in technology.

3.   Conduct of the consumer: improper usage and modifications by the user can be a defense to product liability claims.

4.   Other property rule: a defect that keeps a product for functioning but does not harm other property or cause personal injury is not a basis for a product liability claim.

5.   Preemption: if a state tort claim imposes a standard in conflict with a federal standard, then the federal standard trumps.

(i) Express preemption: a federal statute or regulation expressly states that a state tort claim cannot be brought.

(ii) Implied preemption: ask if a federal statute or regulation creates a safety standard. Then ask if a state tort claim creates a standard inconsistent with the federal standard. If the state tort claim does create an inconsistent standard, then the state tort claim is dismissed.

(iii) Do not confuse the defense of preemption with the use of statutes to establish negligence per se.

F.   Restatement (Third) of Torts: Products Liability

    1.   Adopted more than half the states. A dynamic area so pay attention to your particular instructor about developments.

    2.   Manufacturing defect: strict liability if product does not conform to intended design.

    3.   Design defect: risk-utility test is the sole one with consumer expectations relevant to determining risk or utility of design. Plaintiff must show reasonable alternative design unless design is "manifestly unreasonable."

    4.   Inadequate warning or instruction: foreseeable risk could have been avoided or mitigated through reasonable warning or instructions, where reasonableness depends on the circumstances.

XII.   Reputation Based Torts

A.   The reputation based torts consist of defamation and four individual tort claims that fall under protection of privacy.

B.   Defamation: (i) publication (ii) about the plaintiff (iii) that is defamatory and (iv) results in damages.

    1.   Publication: a communication to a third party other than plaintiff or defendant.

        a.   Publication must have been made either intentionally or negligently.

        b.   If the defendant is the author or the publisher of the communication, then strict liability applies to the other elements of the defamation claim.

        c.   If the defendant is the distributor of the communication, then the distributor must have known or should have known that the communication was defamatory.

        d.   Under federal law, Internet service providers have immunity from defamation claims based on defamatory communications made by users of the service.

    2.   About the plaintiff

a. The subject of the communication can be apparent from the literal words of the communication or from the context of the communication.

b. Group defamation is possible if the individuals who comprise the group are specific and easily ascertainable. General statements about groups are not actionable as defamation.

3. Defamatory: based on a reasonable interpretation of the communication.

4. Damages: depends on the nature of the communication.

a. If spoken (that is slander), then special damages must be shown unless the communication falls into one of four slander per se categories:

i. Serious criminal conduct.

ii. Harm to trade, business, or profession.

iii. Loathsome disease.

iv. Unchastity of a woman.

b. In most jurisdictions, if the communication is written (libel), then general damages are presumed and special damages need not be shown.

c. In some jurisdictions, special damages are required for libel unless

i. the statement is defamatory on its face OR

ii. the statement counts as slander per se.

d. In these latter jurisdictions, libel requiring the showing of special damages is referred to as libel per quod and libel not requiring the showing of special damages is referred to as libel per se.

4. Defenses to defamation

a. Truth: generally a substantial truth standard.

b.   Privileges:

i.   Absolute for public officials and official statements.

ii.   Qualified for references and other contexts in which truthful and open communication is desirable.

iii.   If the defendant has malice, then the privilege is lost.

c.   First Amendment: imposes an additional requirement on the plaintiff

i.   Defendant is public official or public figure: plaintiff must show that defendant has actual malice, i.e. that defendant knew of the falsity of the communication or acted with reckless disregard for its falsity.

ii.   Defendant is from the media and the plaintiff is a private person: liability cannot be strict. Most jurisdictions require the plaintiff to show that the media defendant acted negligently in making the defamatory communication. Some jurisdictions require intent.

C.   Privacy torts

1.   False light. defendant published a statement about the plaintiff that was false.

a.   If the communication is a matter of public concern, then the plaintiff must show actual malice.

2.   Public Disclosure of private facts: defendant (i) publicizes a matter concerning the private life of the plaintiff, (ii) where the matter publicized would be highly offensive to a reasonable person, and (iii) the matter is not of legitimate concern to the public.

a.   Consent of the plaintiff is a defense.

b.   If defendant is a member of the media, then there can be no liability for the publication of truthful information legally obtained unless the state has an interest of the highest order.

3.   Intrusion: defendant intentionally intrudes in a place where the plaintiff has a reasonable expectation of privacy.

    a.   Consent of the plaintiff is a defense.

    b.   If the defendant communicates information obtained from the intrusion, then the defendant has a First Amendment defense if the public interest in the information outweighs the privacy concerns of the plaintiff.

    c.   A third party who obtains the information from the defendant is not liable.

4.   Right of publicity: defendant commercializes the name, likeness or other personal attribute of the plaintiff.

    a.   The Supreme Court has held that there is no First Amendment defense if the defendant takes all commercial value of the plaintiff's publicity.

    b.   Lower courts have found First Amendment protection if the defendant transforms the public attribute of the plaintiff in a creative manner.

XIII.   Business Torts

A.   Misrepresentation: can be intentional or negligent.

1.   Fraud or deceit: (i) a material misrepresentation; (ii) the defendant acted with the requisite scienter; (iii) the defendant intended to induce reliance; (iv) the misrepresentation caused the plaintiff's justifiable reliance; (v) pecuniary damages resulted to the plaintiff.

    a.   Fraud or deceit can be the basis for damages or rescission.

2.   Negligent misrepresentation: (i) a material misrepresentation; (ii) the defendant acted unreasonably in disclosing or investigating the facts represented; (iii) the misrepresentation caused the plaintiff's reasonable and justifiable reliance; (iv) pecuniary damages to the plaintiff.

      a. Negligent misrepresentation is remedied by damages.

B. Injurious Falsehood: (i) a false statement of a kind calculated to damage a pecuniary interest of the plaintiff; (ii) publication to a third party; (iii) malice in the publication; and (iv) special damages suffered by the plaintiff.

C. Intentional Interference with Contract: (i) existence of a valid contract; (ii) knowledge of the valid contract by the defendant; (iii) intent by the defendant to interfere with the valid contract; (iv) interference with the contract caused by the defendant; and (v) damages to the plaintiff.

      1. Justifications: (i) the nature of the defendant's conduct; (ii) the defendant's motive; (iii) the interests of the third party with which the defendant's conduct interferes; (iv) the interests sought to be advanced by the defendant; (v) the social interests in protecting the freedom of action of the defendant and the contractual or economic interests of the third party; (vi) the proximity or remoteness of the defendant's conduct to the interference; and (vii) the relations between the parties.

D. Intentional Interference with Economic Relations: (i) existence of an economic relationship between the plaintiff and a third party that has the possibility of resulting in future economic gain to the plaintiff; (ii) knowledge by the defendant of the existence of the relationship; (iii) intent by the defendant to interfere with the economic relationship; (iv) actual interference; and (v) damages to the plaintiff caused by the interference.

      1. Justifications: same as under intentional interference with contract.

E. Misappropriation: this tort consists of the following five elements to the claim of misappropriation: (i) Plaintiff gathered information at a cost; (ii) Information is time sensitive; (iii) Defendant's use constitutes free riding of plaintiff's effort; (iv) Plaintiff and defendant are direct competitors; and (v) Defendant's free riding would substantially reduce the incentive of plaintiff to gather the information.

XIV. Torts Arising From The Legal Process

A. Malicious Initiation of Civil Proceedings

1. Elements: (1) bringing a civil proceeding against the plaintiff; (2) termination of the proceeding in favor of the plaintiff; (3) absence of a reasonable basis for the proceeding; (4) improper purpose of the party bringing the proceeding; and (5) damages suffered by the plaintiff.

2. Different from Rule 11 Sanctions which are penalties imposed by a judge in a civil proceeding against an attorney who has submitted a frivolous or fraudulent pleading, motion, or other document.

B. Malicious Prosecution

1. Elements: (1) bringing a civil proceeding against the plaintiff; (2) termination of the proceeding in favor of the plaintiff; (3) absence of probable cause for the proceeding; (4) improper purpose of the party bringing the proceeding; and (5) damages suffered by the plaintiff.

2. Existence of immunities will limit the suit.

C. Abuse of Process

1. Elements: (1) initiating a legal process, such as an attachment or an arrest; (2) absence of a reasonable basis for the proceeding; (3) improper purpose of the party bringing the proceeding; and (4) damages suffered by the plaintiff.